Michael Partridge.

Maverick Airman

The Extraordinary Life
of
Frederick Frank Reilly
Minchin

by
Michael J Partridge

ISBN 978-0-9554940-1-7

Published by
The Eastbourne College Arnold Embellishers
Marlborough House, Old Wish Road
Eastbourne BN21 4JY

Printed and bound by
CPI Antony Rowe Ltd
Bumpers Farm, Chippenham
Wiltshire SN14 6LH

Foreword

by Mike O'Connor

The period after the First World War was the romantic age of aviation. Flying had captured the imagination of the general public. Hardly a week went by without another record-breaking flight and pilots such as Amy Johnson, Bert Hinkler and Charles Lindbergh became famous, if not household, names. For many of those flyers who had survived the war, life was an adventure and the risks made up for the mundane peace after the heady excitement and drama of the Great War. However, the reality was quite different, with most struggling to earn a precarious living in the fledgling airlines and other companies that had sprung up. In these pioneering years of aviation many characters stood out as larger than life – sadly many to be lost in risky enterprises.

One of these was Freddie Minchin, an enigmatic individual who during a distinguished RFC/RAF career had reached the rank of lieutenant-colonel and command of a wing, consisting of several squadrons. His courage and leadership qualities were undoubted and during his wartime service he had been awarded a DSO, MC and Bar and a CBE. Tall, handsome and popular, he was however a wayward character, incapable of managing his financial affairs, always in debt and who moved effortlessly from one scrape to another. In order to clear his debts and earn a living he was one of the many who attempted a daring if not dangerous record-breaking flight.

There was none more daunting than the east to west crossing of the Atlantic. The prevailing winds were against you, the weather was frequently poor and unpredictable with little in the way of meteorological forecasting. In addition, aeroplanes and engines were of dubious reliability. If forced to ditch, the odds of survival were slim; indeed as there was virtually no survival equipment and rescue services were non-existent. On such a flight in 1927 Minchin and his two companions joined the long list of aviators who attempted the crossing and disappeared into a watery grave. You get the feeling that Freddie Minchin's life was doomed to end in tragedy.

This excellently researched and absorbing biography brings to life one of the most intriguing and unsung pioneers of British aviation history and I trust the reader enjoys it as much as I have.

Mike O'Connor
East Sussex
2009

Mike O'Connor was born in 1947 and is the son of an RAF pilot. After a number of schools, due to the family moving round RAF postings, he learned to fly at Kidlington in 1967 and joined British European Airways in 1968. After five years flying the Vickers Vanguard, he flew Boeing 707s, 737s, 747s, Tristars, the BAC1-11 and finally, for two years, the Concorde. He retired early in 1998 after some 14,000 flying hours and now devotes much of his spare time to aviation research. His publications include 'Number One in War and Peace: The History of No 1 Squadron', 'In the Footsteps of the Red Baron' (both with Norman L R Franks) and four shorter books on World War One airmen and airfields.

Acknowledgements

I owe a debt of gratitude to many people. In particular I am happy to give heartfelt thanks to my former collaborator Derek O'Connor, whose research skills are second to none. I am sincerely grateful to him for information about the early days of civil aviation, about Minchin's part in it, for his helpful reviews of some of my early chapters, and, not least, his generous permission to use the fruits of his hard work at Colindale, the British Library and elsewhere. Minchin's brother Harry wrote a moving record of the life of the brother whom he and the family called 'Jack' and this has helped to fill many gaps in the story. I must also record my thanks to Robina Pelham Burn, freelance editor, Trevor Henshaw, author of *The Sky their Battlefield*, Peter Skinner, archivist of the Croydon Airport Society, General David Thomson, military historian, and Mike O'Connor, aviation historian and author, who have reviewed my manuscript in whole or part and made many helpful comments.

Many others have helped with information or advice: Debby Andrews of the Centre for Newfoundland Studies, Stefania Arnórsdóttir from Iceland, Ralph Barker, David J Barnes, Lewis Benjamin, the late Chaz Bowyer, the late Jack Bruce, Lynn Bullock, curator of the PPCLI Museum, Owen Clark, Andrew Cormack, Andrew Whitmarsh and P J V Elliott of the RAF Museum, Peter Craig, Tim Dubé of the National Archives of Canada, Teddy Fennelly, Mike Fish of British Aerospace Archives, Hugh Halliday of the Canadian Aviation Historical Society, Ken Harman, Keith Hayward and the late Fred Huntley MBE of BA Archives, Darrell Hillier, Mrs Jan Keohane of the Fleet Air Arm Museum, James Kostuchuk (one time owner of Jack's uniform and medals), Paul Leaman, Rick Leisenring of the Curtiss Museum, Stuart Leslie, the late Mike Marshall, Sqn Ldr Mike Napier RAF (retd), Tom Newman and Ralph Strong of the National Air and Space Museum, Washington, Andy Thomas, Angela Wootton and Stephen Walton of the Imperial War Museum, Theo Wesselink, Richard Whittle and Larry Williamson of the Croydon Airport Society, Nathan Wright, Hugh Yea and John Zabarylo of the Military Collectors' Club of Canada. My apologies also go to anyone whom I may inadvertently have omitted.

The internet perhaps deserves its own thanks.

And my sincere thanks go to my graphic designer, Martin Bannon, for his patience with a never-ending stream of amendments, his professionalism and his unfailing good humour.

Finally, but by no means least, my thanks to my dear wife Sheila who for several years has cheerfully put up with the presence of Jack Minchin in our house, and who has read the manuscript and commented helpfully.

I remain responsible for all errors and omissions.

Michael Partridge

Illustration Credits

The Minchin family at Annagh compiled an album, now lodged with the Imperial War Museum, which records Jack's life from childhood through to his death. It contains numerous rare photographs and a unique collection of press cuttings, personal correspondence and memorabilia. The IWM, supported by the late Brian Minchin, has given me unlimited access to this album. Brian, Harry's son and Jack's nephew, gave me generous access to the letters that Jack wrote from Belgium, France and North Africa to his grandfather and some are reproduced here. Another of Jack's nephews, Denis Minchin, has been most supportive of the project and has provided additional information and photographs about the uncle that he never knew. The Croydon Airport Society, supported by an enthusiastic team of volunteer archivists, has been generous in allowing me to reproduce material from their archives. I have also drawn on the resources of the Eastbourne College archives. Ralph Barker, Trevor Henshaw, Mike O'Connor, the late AJ Jackson, *Flight International*, *The Aeroplane*, the *Illustrated London News* and the National Archives have all been generous in their support. All other identifiable sources have been approached for permission and strenuous efforts have been made to attribute the photographs to the correct sources. I apologise in advance for any errors or omissions and would be glad to hear from anyone who can shed further light on my sources. Any fresh attributions and permissions will be included in a second edition.

All sources, so far as they are known, are listed on pages 161-2.

Contents

Introduction

I suppose I first became aware of Freddie Minchin while still a schoolboy. Certainly on most of my schooldays I must have walked past the plaque which commemorates his life. It was a colleague at Eastbourne College, Richard Walder, who re-awakened my interest when he mentioned that he had found an account of Minchin's Atlantic flight in Ralph Barker's book *Great Mysteries of the Air*. That was in 1998. Then in 2000 Minchin reappeared briefly in my co-authored book *A History of the Eastbourne Aviation Company 1911–1924*.

Once embarked on this project it became clear that, with diligent research, almost every phase of Minchin's life was documented, sometimes very fully. Aviation enthusiasts are a friendly and helpful lot and I owe much to them. It should also be recorded that, while there was any amount of primary research material to be found at, for example, the National Archives, the Imperial War Museum and the RAF Museum, much of the secondary material, often published by fellow aviators but also by his brother Harry, is sometimes of doubtful accuracy.

Casual readers will find in this book an extraordinarily detailed record of the life of a man who epitomized the brave spirit of those who fought in and survived the 'war to end wars'. World War One and aviation buffs, and many others, will I hope enjoy it. We shall be meeting a man who survived the horrors of Second Ypres and flew with distinction in two of the less well-known battlefields of the Great War, Egypt and Macedonia. Promoted Lieutenant Colonel, he was awarded almost every decoration short of a VC. His second self, the irresponsible, volatile, charismatic 'Jack' Minchin, is there to leaven the mix. So in some respects the Minchin story becomes an exercise in human psychology, though I am the least qualified to conduct any such analysis and have refrained from attempting to do so. I suppose that wars bring out such characters and not all are equipped to return to the mundane ways of peacetime. Here was a man with more than his share of talents and of frailties; a man of whom his family, his school, his regiments and the Royal Air Force can be proud.

I am tempted to think that his old school recorded the most perceptive as well as touching summation of his career:

There are those who count Atlantic flights mere recklessness and their victims foolhardy adventurers. Be that as it may, the sheer courage demanded for the attempt deserves a tribute. In so far as courage, skill and experience can command success in such an undertaking, Minchin was as likely to succeed as any man living, and had he done so, he would have been acclaimed a national hero. Though he had some of the defects, as well as the virtues, of the dare-devil type of character, all who knew him were attracted to him; and while they mourn his death, they feel that the manner of it was worthy of him and worthy of his school.

In 1930 a memorial window was erected on the north wall of a classroom building at Eastbourne College that Minchin would have used during his schooldays. The inscription on the plaque below the window states:

The window above this tablet commemorates
FREDERICK FRANK MINCHIN
(School House 1905-8)
Late Lieut-Colonel Royal Air Force, C.B.E., D.S.O., M.C. and bar,
who on 31 August 1927 with two companions set out in the
aeroplane St. Raphael to cross the Atlantic and passed
out of the sight of men.

Chapter One

Setting the Scene

It was in 1927 that a number of brave, possibly foolhardy, aviators, stimulated by Lindbergh's epic transatlantic flight in June, attempted the more dangerous east to west crossing of the Atlantic by air. Five lives were lost and not one succeeded in the attempt. One of the most distinguished of these was an Anglo-Irishman, Frederick Frank Reilly Minchin, Lt Col RAF (retired), known as 'Jack' to his family and 'Freddie' or 'Dan' to his intimates in the world of aviation. On 31 August he set out, accompanied by Captain Leslie Hamilton MBE DFC, a World War One ace, and by the Princess Loewenstein-Wertheim, to become the first to make this crossing by aeroplane. That they failed is a matter of history.

The course of events that led to this glorious failure centre around the delightful, wayward personality of the main protagonist, 'Jack' Minchin. He was a man of extremes, of extraordinary achievement, and of abject failure. All who knew him tell of his charm, his good looks, his bravery and of his capacity for friendship.

At Sandhurst, his maverick character, under the influence of a group of the wilder cadets, was soon to get him into trouble. Months later he was required to resign his commission in the Connaught Rangers as a result of another ill-judged misdemeanour. He was regularly in debt and as regularly bailed out by his grandfather. As one of the pioneering airmen, he had learned to fly in 1912 while a serving officer with the Connaught Rangers. He was a natural aviator.

Sent by his family to Canada, he appeared to walk away from his responsibilities to a newly formed aviation company.

Brave to a degree, his war service, spent in the purgatory of the trenches of the Ypres Salient and in the air in France and Belgium, the Middle East and India, was exemplary but unsung. At least his superiors in the Royal Flying Corps and the Royal Air Force recognised his merits.

He emerged from the war in 1919 an acting Lieutenant Colonel, with the award of a CBE, DSO, MC and Bar and three mentions-in-despatches. Accepting a permanent commission as Squadron Leader, he soon resigned, apparently fearing the tedium of peacetime service flying.

Yet he was evidently destined for high rank, possibly even Air rank. The award of a CBE at his age was a clear signal. In the post-war RAF List, he was immediately below Tedder and above Portal and Leigh-Mallory. Flying was in his blood and was his talent. After the war and after some unsatisfactory employment in India, he joined the embryonic civil aviation industry as a pilot, flying the 'bus routes' from Croydon to Paris, Cologne and other European capitals. Easily bored and eager for challenges, he volunteered for a variety of proving flights, engine tests and the exploration of inaugural routes.

On the other side of the coin was his alter ego, the weak, easily-led, maverick 'Jack' Minchin. Irresponsible in money matters to an extreme, he found fascination in the company and friendship of men with far greater financial means than his own and whose morality was often to be doubted. His good nature and natural naïvety would judge people at face value and fail to see them as the wastrels that they often were.

After the war, on the boat home from India, he lost his savings and his war gratuity playing cards. Arriving in London virtually penniless, he chose to stay at the Cavendish Hotel in Jermyn Street, a place notorious for the raffish type of person who frequented it. Marrying a beautiful young socialite, both he and she soon found that he could not afford to keep her in the luxury to which she was accustomed. They parted, shortly to divorce. The downhill slide continued, until in 1924 he was destitute and was adjudged bankrupt.

The story of the life of 'Jack' Minchin is one of extraordinary heroism, leadership and achievement in war and in the earliest days of aviation; of a man blessed with looks, charm and personal charisma; and of a man who fatally found easy acquaintances of the wrong sort a swift route to financial ruin. It is a story worth telling.

Chapter Two

Childhood Days

The Minchins of Annagh[1], also the Minchins of Busherstown, both of County Tipperary, were descended from a family of farmers in the village of Wyck Rissington in Gloucestershire, some four miles south of Stow-on-the-Wold, whose history goes back to Tudor and Jacobean times. Captain Charles Minchin of the Parliamentary Army purchased the Annagh estate in 1669, having already acquired the Busherstown estates near Moneygall by Royal grant from Charles II under the Act of Settlement of 1662.

It was around 1815-22 that the new Annagh Lodge was built in the parish of Kilbarron, three miles from Puckane. This was the 'Annagh' that subsequent generations of Minchins would regard as home. The Minchins of Annagh appear to have been humane landlords, operating a

Annagh

---

[1] Annagh was a 400 acre holding in the parish of Kilbarron-Terryglass near to Thurles in County Tipperary.

policy of granting favourable leases to tenants throughout the nineteenth century. Jack's grandfather, Falkiner John, and his father, Frederick Falkiner, the 'Old General', and in due course his brother Harry[2] all farmed the Annagh estates. The Minchins of Annagh were a part of that Anglo-Irish land-owning aristocracy which provided an unending stream of soldiers, sailors, Members of Parliament and administrators for the British crown. Brother Harry refers to them as the 'old, out-at-elbow gentry of good breeding'.

Falkiner John (c.1843–1916) was, in the words of his grandson Harry, Jack's elder brother:

A typical old country gentleman with the accent on the gentleman; a noble, intellectual, tender-hearted, gentle-mannered aristocrat of a type that is now alas extinct. Respected and loved by everybody, he was the soul of honour, deeply religious. He was the main prop not only of his own family but also of the district around...... [as children] *we grew to love Annagh and to adore our grandfather with that deep love and respect which never fades away.*

Frederick Falkiner, Minchin's father and Falkiner John's second son (there were also three daughters), was born in 1860. He was a regular soldier in the Royal Regiment of Artillery and, as his elder brother had died in 1909, he inherited the Annagh estates when his father died in 1916. When his own second son, the subject of this book, was born on 16 June 1890, Frederick Falkiner was a Captain stationed in Madras, India. By 1911 he had reached the rank of full Colonel and was Chief Inspector of Artillery Ordnance at Woolwich. He continued to serve until 1918 when he retired on health grounds as a Major General.

Minchin's early years were spent in India under the care, as was usual for young Europeans of his age, of an Indian ayah, a nurse or nanny, and he saw comparatively little of his parents. As a young child his legs were deformed, probably due to a mild form of rickets, and he spent a lot of time confined to a 'lie-down' perambulator; later he had to wear

---

[2] In the mid 1930s, as a consequence of an economic war between Great Britain and Ireland, Harry sold most of the Annagh estates to the Land Commission, keeping about 50 acres around the house. Subsequent to the Second World War he sold Annagh Lodge and the remainder of the estate and moved into a house on the estate, a former hunting lodge called Murroughboro'. In 2002 Annagh, with 170 acres, was offered for sale by Dublin agents for 1.3M Euros (c.£900,000).

Harry, Jack and Vi in India   Aged nine

Jack on Copper Knob at Annagh

iron splints to support his legs. But by the age of six or seven he had outgrown these handicaps and was tall and slim for his age.

In 1898, with his father stationed in Ceylon, his mother Marjorie brought the children home to England. They took a house in Bedford, where the two small boys attended Bedford Grammar School as day pupils. Then in 1903, with the father now posted to command the Royal Arsenal at Woolwich, the family moved into a house at 139 Shooters Hill Road, Blackheath. Minchin was sent to a preparatory school there called Stratheden House where he soon exhibited an extraordinary capacity for making friends. As his brother Harry later recalled:

> ...this was partly explained by his very good looks, by his charm
> of manner and also by a simplicity of character which took people
> at their own valuation and accepted facts on their superficial
> appearance. He made friends of almost everybody he met and
> almost everybody wanted to be his friend.

His best friends, however, remained his brother Harry (Henry Falkiner), and his sister Vi (Violet Marjorie). Vi was the eldest, born in 1887, while Harry was the middle child, born in 1889. The prevailing rules of inheritance meant that Harry, as the elder son, would become heir to the family estates. In due course this would have significant implications for Minchin.

Minchin's mother, herself the daughter of a General in the British army, died in August 1904 when he was fourteen, and his father spent no fewer than seven years on duty overseas in Ceylon, South Africa and India during Minchin's formative years. His father married for a second time in September 1905 one Caroline Royds Lloyd of Astwick Manor in Hertfordshire, always known within the family as Lena. Harry's view of this marriage was pungent, and more than a little snobbish:

> Our stepmother was not a lady in the strict sense of the word, but
> her parents were rich, and she had moved in the rich, smart, semi-
> county circles which looked down on the old out-at elbow gentry
> of good breeding. Jack had no home now but was used as a kind of
> show specimen in the second rate country houses our stepmother
> enjoyed showing him off in.

It seems probable that Minchin felt alienated from his father, even unloved.

In January 1905 the fourteen year old boy was sent as a boarder to School House at Eastbourne College, which was at that time a modest south coast public school of some 160–170 pupils. The school was one of those many fee-paying schools established in the mid-nineteenth century to provide 'for the education of the sons of Noblemen and Gentlemen', as the original prospectus had it. Minchin was probably classed as 'delicate' and thus his boarding in a salubrious seaside town would have been seen as a sensible move. A fellow pupil who also joined School House in the Michaelmas term of 1905 was one Vernon Brown, later Air Commodore Sir Vernon Brown, CB, OBE, who would re-enter Minchin's life briefly some twenty-two years later.

Following his mother's early death, Minchin was placed under the informal guardianship of an uncle, Lt Col Henry Abbott, late of the Indian Army. The Colonel was his mother's brother and lived in retirement in Eastbourne in a house overlooking the school grounds until his death in 1914. This was Burleigh House, 20 Grange Road, a building since acquired by the school as a day-boy house and named Reeves. Mrs Abbott died in 1908 and the Colonel appears to have had limited influence on his nephew's teenage years. Indeed, after his mother's death, the most important influence on the boy's early life was his grandfather, Falkiner John, hundreds of miles distant at Annagh, who was the one steadying force that rescued him from many a scrape.

Harry described his brother:

Picture to yourself this lad, six foot two or so, dark, terribly handsome, greeny brown eyes, with a most disarming smile and perfect teeth, slim, broad-shouldered, shy and yet self-reliant in a daredevil, reckless way. Seldom speaking and yet when he did, coming out with some very pungent remark, not the result of brainwork, but of an extraordinary naïve way of looking at life. He was gifted with a most elusive, indescribable charm and was of course irresistible to both men and women, particularly to women.

Jack Minchin aged 15

7

The Eastbourne College XV of 1907, Minchin standing right

1909, Minchin (far left) winning the 100 yards race on College Field

The young Rugby player

Minchin was far from being a model pupil at Eastbourne. Indeed he soon began to display the wayward personality that remained with him all his life, while simultaneously being a sound, courageous performer on the sports field. Six foot two or three in height (a tall figure of a boy in an era when few men exceeded six foot), Jack was already a slim, exceptionally good-looking lad with, as revealed in one group photograph, a mischievous grin. A sporting report records his weight as 10 stone 11lb. A fine athlete, he played cricket for the school without significant success, winning his Second XI colours; he also won his colours for gym and was, as a sprinter and jumper, Victor Ludorum in

9

1908. He won his 'Stag', or XV colours, as a brave, dashing, if eccentric, wing threequarter in both 1907 and 1908. Indeed a report[3] on the match against Christ's Hospital in 1907 makes fascinating reading:

> . . .*Carter set Minchin going for the corner flag. He out-raced the opposition, crossed their line without mishap, and then, with Hibernian levity, proceeded to gambol about within a yard of the dead ball line, while they had shots at him one by one; and we, players and spectators alike, adjured him to ground the ball in the name of whatever god came handiest. This, in process of time, he did, and we led by three points until the interval.*

Another match report, this time with Brighton College the opponents, included the comments:

> …*still fiercer tackles abounded from half time onwards. One such tackle by Minchin has certainly left memories behind it – it was the best thing he ever did…*

His end of season report stated that he was:

> *A much improved wing three. He began with a straight run for the corner flag, but now has developed other methods of getting tries, and has even been known to drop a goal. His defence is patchy. If a dare-devil tackle has obviously to be done, he is more than likely to do it . . .but never does he seem to anticipate the tactics of his opponents.*

According to Harry, his brother became 'a perfect daredevil and . . . the leader of the wild section of the school'. Academically his education suffered. In 1908 he failed to pass the entry examination for Sandhurst.

---

[3] *The Eastbournian,* 14 December 1907

Chapter Three

The Connaught Rangers

Aged 18

Leaving Eastbourne in the summer of 1908, a period at a crammers enabled him to take the Sandhurst qualifying examination. As there were more vacancies than usual, he was in 1909 accepted on the qualifying examination alone. He represented the Royal Military College at rugby and played against the Royal Naval College, Greenwich, for whom Harry turned out as a forward. At Sandhurst, according to Harry:

> *His extraordinary personal charm combined with his reckless daredevil spirit made him tremendously popular with the more 'sporting' members of the cadets. Unfortunately for Jack, these were not the most desirable companions for one who was not well off and who could seldom say no. The lad got into several scrapes for wildness and eventually Dad had to go down to Sandhurst to see the Commandant and Jack was let off with a good lecturing and a 'confined to barracks.'*

Presentation of colours at the Curragh, 1912. Minchin circled (without cap)

Although we do not know what precisely were his misdemeanours, it was only on the personal intervention of Colonel Minchin, his father, that the Commandant was persuaded to commute his punishment.

In December 1909 he passed out of Sandhurst, 108th out of 138, and was gazetted in October 1910 to the 2nd Battalion of the Connaught Rangers, stationed at the Curragh in County Tipperary, Ireland.

The Connaught Rangers was a proud Irish regiment. Raised as the 88th Regiment of Foot in Connaught in 1793, it had fought with distinction in the Peninsular War of 1807-1814, distinguishing itself at every battle or siege from Talavera through to Toulouse. It gained further distinction in the Crimea, in the Zulu War of 1877-79 and in the South African War of 1899-1902. Minchin was joining one of the élite regiments of the British army. A 1912 photograph of the regiment's officers and their ladies at a colours presentation ceremony shows a hatless Minchin in

regimental blues, with a brother officer's arm around his shoulders.

At the Curragh, Minchin's wayward character again led him astray. Extraordinarily popular, he demonstrated his talent for making friends with the wrong people. He joined a group of wealthy and dashing young subalterns with a generally devil-may-care outlook on life. One account suggests that he kept a string of polo ponies. 'Bird' Fenton, a brother officer in the regiment, dubbed him 'the longest, blackest and slackest thing in Kildare'. He was soon in bad odour with Colonel Abercrombie, his commanding officer, and he ran into debt. In a gallant attempt to get out of trouble, he bought a horse at Bannagher for £20 which he trained and entered for the Irish Grand Military Steeplechase. He started favourite and had he won, would have cleared £150 to £200 and been able to pay his debts. Sadly the horse fell at the penultimate fence when well ahead of the field. A furious grandfather Minchin paid off his grandson's debts.

Late in 1912 Minchin, together with Harry, who was by now an officer in the Royal Navy, decided to apply to learn to fly. Harry, however, was sent on a Naval gunnery course while Minchin applied and was refused by his Colonel. He then applied for a month's leave and, while leaving his address as Annagh, actually went to Eastbourne and began a course of training at the flying school[4] there. This had been opened on the marshes to the east of the town in 1911 by an enthusiastic pioneer airman, Frederick Bernard Fowler, who was busily designing and building his own aircraft, operating joy-rides off the sea front and teaching tyros to fly on two-seater Blériots and Boxkites. Assisted by a New Zealander, Joseph Joel Hammond, Fowler taught Minchin to fly. Brother Harry had provided an indemnity, fortunately not needed, of £100 against Minchin smashing one of Fowler's aircraft.

The Bristol Boxkite was a refined Henri Farman biplane, built as a trainer by the British and Colonial Aeroplane Company[5] from 1910 onwards. Looking like a large and unwieldy kite, it was usually powered by a 50hp Gnome rotary engine located behind the pilot. Popular as a trainer at British flying schools, its great advantage was that it was a friendly and safe aircraft. Minchin left no record of his time at Eastbourne, but fortunately Douglas Iron, later Air Commodore, who gained his certificate at the Eastbourne airfield a year after Minchin, has left a graphic record of what it was like to learn to fly there on a Boxkite. Writing some sixty years later, he recalled the experience with precision:

> Our three Boxkites had neither dual control nor instruments of any kind, although there was an oil pulsator situated near one's left foot, to assure us that pure castor oil was still flowing back and forth. Ailerons were still of the single-acting variety, and hung down until sufficient speed had been gained over the ground to make them operate; and the rotary engine had no means to throttle it down to reduce its revolutions. It was a matter of full out or stop, until one got the hang of it. At no time did the trainee, sitting on the leading edge of the lower plane with his legs round his instructor, touch the controls, although he was allowed to place his hand over that of his

---

[4] This was the Eastbourne Aviation Company Ltd.
[5] This became the Bristol Aeroplane Company in 1920.

mentor on the joystick. However, with a top speed of about 45 mph, one had plenty of time to call to mind the simple drill, which went like this: keep the elevator well down when getting off, and never let it get above the horizon in level flight. During turns, watch the short length of white tape attached to the elevator structure, as it should always stream towards one. On the other hand, should it show signs of veering off towards the left or right, then you are either slipping IN or OUT and something must be done about it without delay. On landing, NEVER 'lose' one's engine, for the gliding angle of the Boxkite is very steep indeed; which is an understatement. When it was time to go solo, the instructor would nip down from his high and exposed perch, fix you with his eye and indicate that you should take over and, with knees knocking, you did so.

To gain his Royal Aero Club certificate, Minchin would have been required to carry out two five-kilometre solo flights and weave figures of eight at a height of roughly 300 feet, before landing the brake-less Boxkite with engine dead and rolling it to rest within fifty yards of a chosen spot. Many believed that flying was akin to riding a horse, and certainly Jack was an accomplished horseman. Whatever the reasons, he took to flying like a duck to water and, passing his test on a Boxkite early in 1913, the award of his RAeC certificate (no 419) came perhaps two weeks later on 13 February 1913.

Unfortunately for him, there was a case of embezzlement at the Curragh while he was at Eastbourne and he was needed as a witness. When his Colonel wired to Annagh to recall him from leave, he was told that he was not there and that they did not know his whereabouts. When Minchin eventually returned, he was put under open arrest. Quite apart from travelling to England while his leave required him to remain in Ireland, it is highly improbable that his training at Eastbourne could have been completed within a month. Consequently he had probably overstayed his leave in order to complete his flying training.

Harry tried manfully to save his brother's career, pleading with his Colonel and a General von Dunop at the War Office who was a friend of the boys' father. All to no avail. Colonel Abercrombie was not prepared to consider a posting to another Connaught Rangers battalion, even

Brother Harry

The RAeC certificate photograph

to another regiment. Unfortunately Minchin's father was in India throughout this period and could not bring his influence to bear. He was allowed to resign his commission, effective 6 February 1913, and his grandfather again paid off his debts. His RAeC Certificate was granted just a week after his resignation.

Protracted family conferences followed and, largely at his stepmother Lena's instigation, Minchin, like many family black sheep, was shipped off to the Colonies, in this case Canada, with very little money, a small monthly allowance and some letters of introduction. The two brothers met at Eastbourne, walked together and pledged each other's loyalty; they then had a farewell oyster supper together. 'One of the most tragic days of all my life,' Harry was to say later. He gave Jack all his spare cash and they parted. The next day Minchin bought a small present and posted it to Harry. 'Though', as Harry said, 'God knows he could not spare the money.'

Chapter Four

In Canada

Soon Minchin was in Winnipeg, Manitoba, where he tried a variety of jobs while continuing to hanker after a role in the emergent field of aviation. During 1913, he wrote a number of articles for the Canadian press under the byline: 'F F R Minchin, Aviator, Special to the Free Press' which sought to infect readers with his own enthusiasm for aviation and to stimulate interest in the formation of a Canadian flying corps.

Eventually, in March 1914, there was formed the Western Canadian Aviation Company Limited (Winnipeg), 'to promote and exploit aviation for commercial, recreative and other purposes', with capital stock of $10,000, divided into 100 shares, each selling for $100. The incorporators were Frederick F R Minchin, William V Miles, Charles S A Rogers, George A Hughes and James A Kesketh.

On 1 June, under the headline 'Aviation Company', the *Manitoba Free Press* reported that W C Powers, President of the company, and F F R Minchin hoped to have a hydroplane or flying boat in operation by July 1914[6] . In fact the company purchased two 'rattletrap' machines, Curtiss Pusher 1910 types, one a waterplane. The landplane had been

A Curtiss pusher

---

[6] There is some confusion here because Frank Ellis in his *Canada's Flying Heritage* states that it was a partnership between Clair G Horton and William J Robertson that purchased the two used pusher biplanes, one a hydroplane, from the Curtiss Company.

used at exhibitions and its fabric was defaced with a myriad of scribbled signatures.

Harwood Steele, Historian to the Canadian Arctic Expedition of 1925, writing an obituary following Minchin's death in 1927, recalled their days together in Winnipeg in 1913 and 1914 and captures with great affection the character of his 23 year old friend:

He is partly Irish, though he says in his quaint way that he is not considered so by the true-blue Paddy because his family, which is prominent in Tipperary, has only been in Ireland since the days of Queen Elizabeth. He talks little – when we lunched together in the Royal Aero Club last March, having seen nothing of each other since the war – he said barely a word. His humor, though lit by sparkling comment, is the humor of action rather than of words, and his shrewd smile takes the place of noisier mirth.

All the same, with his abnormal height of six feet three or more, his dark head and eyes, his original methods and his brilliant courage, Jack cannot help being exactly the present day counterpart of the bygone Irish soldier-adventurer, a modern Charles O'Malley. He was just the same when he ambled into Winnipeg in 1912 [actually 1913], with a letter of introduction to my father and the intention of knocking about Canada. His favourite bit of poetry in those days – and I suspect the only one he knew – was well-known:

My father cared little for shot and shell;
He laughed at death and dangers.
He'd storm the very gates of hell
With a company of the Rangers.

The Rangers were of course Jack's old regiment.

I saw Minchin almost every day for almost two years. A caged eagle, fretting constantly for flight, his heart was in the air. He loyally tried his hand at desperately tame jobs, but was a very square peg in a very round hole. Narrow little associates could not understand why he hated book-keeping and gloomily prophesied his utter failure. They did not know that the winged steed Pegasus was never meant to be a cart-horse.

He was a fighter then, just as he is now. He licked the devil out of a man who laughed at his Old Country manner. We had happy times, for all their tameness. Long walks and tea at McAllister's, a little rendezvous now defunct, were our chief dissipations, as neither of us was wealthy. The greatest excitement we ever shared was the arrival of the tumbledown aeroplane purchased for Jack's aviation company. Crowds flocked to the tent to gaze in awe at it, as at some hideous monster in its lair, while they regarded Minchin, who was willing to go up in so crazy a contraption, as men look on gods.

Those days were brightened everywhere by Jack's quiet humour. I had a bicycle. Though no longer a child, Jack rode it for amusement, his lanky legs reaching easily to the ground, even when he sat in the saddle. The janitor of our apartment house had in his care a cherished patch of green grass. Around this patch centred a fascinating game. The game was to ride the bicycle at full speed across the sacred grass whenever its guardian wasn't looking. Jack excelled at this recreation, and thoroughly enjoyed it, as the janitor constantly tried to stop us with marvellous profanity, and often with physical force. He led a dog's life.

I clearly remember an evening spent table-rapping. About a dozen people, Jack among them, tried to raise the spirits. Also among them was a young lady who took such matters so seriously that she demanded a profound reverence and solemnity. The results on this occasion were wonderful. We got Father Damien, Cleopatra, La Pompadour and all kinds of celebrities of whom some of us had never heard, though all were genuine antiques. They talked to us for hours, revealing recollections of their lives on earth that were not merely marvellously vivid and accurate to the last degree, but sometimes very racy. They specialized in good advice, especially to the girls. 'Tell Molly that she must not flirt in public' or 'I advise Jean to take some of the paint off her face.' It was impossible to detect any trickery. Everybody was impressed. The enthusiastic young lady was even delighted. Jack merely smiled. Afterwards, he confessed his guilt, proving that, thanks to very long, strong, hands, he could work the oracle without detection.

Next, on 29 June 1914, the *Manitoba Free Press*, under the headline *Thrills A-Plenty at Kirkfield Park, July 1*, announced a race between a

Curtiss aeroplane, a motorcycle and an automobile – a feature of a presentation sponsored by the Western Aerial and Automobile Association. An advertisement for the event mentioned 'exhibition flying by daring British aviator.' This sounded promising, until the same newspaper on 2 July headlined its article 'Race Meeting Proves Distinct Frost – 2000 disappointed at Kirkfield Park when airman did not appear.' Minchin had sent a message stating that a serious accident to his machine had prevented his appearance. *The Winnipeg Tribune* on the same day was more explicit:

> *2000 People Disappointed. Aviator Minchin who was supposed to give a fifteen minute flight and later on compete against a motorcycle and an automobile sent his regards stating that an accident to his machine had proved to be more serious than at first regarded . . . As the aeroplane flight was the main attraction of the day, a large crowd left the grounds after waiting some fifteen minutes for the aviator to show up.*

This episode shows Minchin at his most irresponsible. With war visibly imminent, he seems to have deserted the new aviation company for which he had been at such pains to find subscribers. He had managed to raise $10,000 and, without him, the venture was more than likely to have to be wound up.

Chapter Five

Princess Patricia's Canadian Light Infantry

On 11 August 1914, with war in Europe declared, Major Andrew Hamilton Gault, who had served in South Africa with the Royal Highlanders of Canada, travelled to Ottawa to propose to the Canadian Minister of Defence, Colonel Sam Hughes, the formation of a regiment composed of ex-regulars which he would pay for and serve in himself. His contribution was $100,000. Her Royal Highness, the Princess Patricia, daughter of the Duke of Connaught, then Governor General of Canada, agreed to give her name to the regiment. Recruiting posters for this brand new volunteer regiment, Princess Patricia's Canadian Light Infantry (PPCLI), soon appeared in major cities, including Winnipeg. The Duke's Military Secretary, Lt Col Francis Farquhar, DSO, became its first commanding officer and was to be twice mentioned in despatches before being killed in action near St Eloi in March 1915.

By 19 August, three thousand men had applied, most with previous service in British or Canadian militia or regular forces, and 90 per cent had been born in Britain. One group of volunteers had even hi-jacked a train to take them to Ottawa, while others had ridden to the nearest station, hitched their horses to a rail and caught the first train travelling eastwards. During the war, 229 officers and 4,857 other ranks served in the regiment's one battalion and won three VCs and 366 other decorations. The Frezenberg Memorial, a tribute to the officers and other ranks who gave their lives in the Ypres Salient, was erected in 1957. It stands near the village of Westhoek, some three miles east of Ypres, just north of the Menin Road and 500 yards from where on 8 May 1915 the Patricias made their heroic stand on the Frezenberg Ridge. The Menin Gate at Ypres bears the names of 557 Patricias who have no known grave.

Out of the 3000 men who volunteered, 1098 'Originals' were selected, including Minchin, who was commissioned after a fortnight. At the inaugural parade in Lansdowne Park, Ottawa, Her Royal Highness,

PPCLI Officers, Lansdowne Park, Ottawa, August 1914 (Minchin standing, right)
Standing: Capt ASAM Adamson, Lt LT Bennett, Major JWH McKinery, Major CB Keenan (MO),
Lt CE Crabbe, Major RT Pelly, Capt DFB Gray, Lt HW Niven, Major AH Gault, Lt Col FD Farquhar,
Capt HC Buller, Lt E Christie, Lt CA Wake, Major JD Hay Shaw, Capt CF Smith, Major CQ Court,
Lt DE Cameron, Major JS Ward, Lt FF Minchin
Seated: Capt McDougal, Lt HE Sulivan, Lt BF Bainsmith, Lt JL Carr, Lt F Fitzgerald, Lt TM Papineau,
Lt PV Cornish, Lt MS DeBay, Lt CH Price, Lt FL Eardley-Wilmot

Princess Patricia, presented to the regiment a colour which she had herself designed and made. It was not an official College of Heralds approved regimental colour, but, christened 'Ric-A-Dam-Doo' by the regiment, would be carried into every battle in which they fought. They marched past to the strains of *Blue Bonnets over the Border* played by the Edmonton Pipe Band. The aviation company was easily forgotten.

A photograph of the PPCLI officers taken on 27 August 1914 shows Minchin standing a little apart from the others in a borrowed Canadian pattern tunic. He was ecstatically happy to be back in uniform.

On Friday 28 August the regiment boarded the liner *Megantic* at Montreal, bound for England. They sailed the next morning but at Quebec found that they were not allowed to cross the Atlantic except in convoy. No escort was available and so they disembarked and camped at Levis. Here on 9 September Minchin penned the following letter to his grandfather, to whom he would write regularly throughout the war years until the latter's death in May 1916. He always addressed grandfather Minchin as 'GP'.

My dear old GP,

I am back to it again. I don't think there is anything like being an army officer after all. I am very delighted and our Colonel [Francis Farquhar, DSO] is one of the very best.

We have been unexpectedly held here for two weeks now and we expected to go straight out. The trouble was that they could get nobody to escort us. Did you get my letter telling you all about the regiment, how I enlisted & got my commission.

The battalion is coming on very fast, the men are fine. Only some of the officers who got in through political pull are rather a drag on us, and are very inefficient.

I am off for dinner now so I must dash on and say good bye for the present. We are I imagine going to Aldershot and could you tell Aunt Louise that any very warm underclothing she can lay her hands on I will buy from her, as I shall want it in Germany.

Yours ever

Jack

After a month of training, and fearing that the war might be over before they arrived, they sailed again on 27 September on the *Royal George* and, after three weeks at sea, arrived on 18 October at Bustard Camp on Salisbury Plain. There they were inspected by King George V. Major Hamilton Gault, the regiment's founder, formally handed over the regiment to his service.

On 15 November, the Patricias moved to Winchester to join four British regular battalions who had just returned from India to form the 80th Infantry Brigade, part of the 27th Division of the new V Corps under General Sir Herbert Plumer. Jack wrote again to his grandfather on 19 November from Winchester:

My dear old GP,

How are you getting along. I'm so sorry I have not written to you for such a long time but we have moved to this place and received orders to be able to march out in two hours time.

What about the shooting at Holywell [7]? How is it getting on? Is it let? If not, we are close to it here. I think it would be quite possible for me to go over and see the place, I have never been there yet.

I have had a very cheery letter from Harry, and one from Vi [his sister]. When I come back wounded, I am going to get her to nurse me.

We are being put into a regular division of troops from India.

I must end now, but I will write soon.

Jack.

On 22 November he wrote again:

My dear old GP,

How are you. I got my waterproof thanks very much, but my revolver I have had to requisition for through the stores and it is debited in my pay. They are charging me 4£ for it. I have also had to buy a rucksack to carry kit in as we have all been ordered to get them.

Holywell

---

[7] Holywell, near Soberton in Hampshire, was the English home of the Minchins, built in about 1772 and purchased by Humphrey Minchin when he became an MP in the English Parliament.

We may be here for some time I hear and it will be very dull, unless they have another scare as they did before we came. About four of the regiments here were ordered to go to the east coast in two hours notice and when they got there it was cancelled and they had to come back. Apparently they got wind of some scheme to land or the German fleet broke loose or something.

I have heard from Gwen Lloyd [probably a relative of his stepmother, Lena, who was a Lloyd], *or Bennett as she is now, also Harry and Aunt Minnie* [one of his father's sisters].

No news about the flying corps.

I must end now.

Jack.

Minchin had evidently already applied for a transfer to the Royal Flying Corps. The RFC, formed on 13 April 1912, was at this date in its infancy. In support of the British Expeditionary Force (BEF), the RFC initially deployed just four squadrons, Nos. 2, 3, 4 and 5, comprising a total of 105 officers, 755 airmen, 63 aircraft of various types and 95 vehicles. Most pilots were officers seconded from parent regiments or corps, supplemented by a number of NCO pilots. The RFC's first flight of the war, an armed reconnaissance, was carried out on 19 August 1914 by a Blériot monoplane[8] of 3 Squadron and a BE2b of 4 Squadron.

Minchin was getting bored waiting for his war to start and within a week, on 29 November, was writing again to his grandfather:

My dear old GP,

I ran down to Holywell today I could not shoot of course as it is Sunday but I went over the house which is in very good order and quite nice; the gardens are well kept and the man there is a very civil man.

I sent on your letter to Mr Gunner and he wrote today and asked me to shoot on Thursday next but I don't expect I shall be able to. The poor man has lost his son in the Navy on the Bulwark which went down at Sheerness. He has another son in the Hampshire

---

[8] Piloted by Philip Joubert de la Ferté, later Air Chief Marshal Sir Philip Joubert de la Ferté, KCB, CMG, DSO.

Yeomanry in the same division as we are. He is living in a hotel in Winchester.

We hope to go to the front about the 8th of next month. The officials at the War Office want me to go to the Canadian Flying Corps. The Colonel is very angry about it. He says it arouses his worst passions. He is going to see what he can do for me.

Yours ever,

Jack.

At last, on 21 December 1914, the Patricias embarked at Southampton in the *SS Cardiganshire* for the crossing to Le Havre, four long months since they had left Ottawa. They had endured the wet, the cold and the mud of the worst English autumn in living memory, almost certainly under canvas. Conditions in France were no better but at least they were now, at last, where they wanted to be.

After another wet, cold night at Le Havre, they boarded a train made up of tightly packed boxcars, with standing room only for many, bound for St Omer. The short journey took twenty-four hours of great discomfort. They then marched towards their billets which were to be in and around the village of Blaringhem, some ten miles south-east of St Omer. Unfortunately their guide for the latter part of the march lost his way and at 1500hrs it was discovered that they had gone two miles out of their way and had to retrace their steps. They stayed in Blaringhem for a few days and enjoyed a Christmas dinner of bully beef. They were not amused.

Soon after Christmas, the Patricias were sent to bolster the Hazebrouck defensive line where they spent the last week of the year digging trenches into the sodden soil of Flanders. On 1 January 1915 they were inspected by Sir John French. Then on 5 January they marched forward into Belgium, through Dickebusch, towards Ypres, bound for the Allied front line at St Eloi, some two miles to the south of Ypres, where they relieved the 53rd Regiment of the 32nd French Division. The trenches were mere ditches dug in a sea of mud and offered little protection from shells or bullets. In some parts the water was waist deep and the trenches regularly collapsed due to lack of revetting. Unburied bodies lay to the front and rear and the area was infested with rats. All movement had to be effected by night because the enemy was on higher ground and there were at that time no communication trenches to the rear.

There was a shortage of boots and many Patricias had worn through the soles of theirs. Sickness due to exposure and the new phenomenon of trench foot (with which the medical staff had not yet learned to cope) was high.

On 7 January 1915, the regiment's first day in the front line, they lost two men killed. During the following six weeks, they suffered severe casualties and, together with high losses due to sickness, they were at one time 400 men under strength. Among these was Minchin. He wrote again to his grandfather at Annagh on 29 January from No 1 General Hospital at Le Havre:

My dear old GP,

How are you. I feel very ashamed of myself for not having written before but there is no news worth telling you. I have been in this hospital a week, very much against my wishes but they moved me down here. I had to go sick because I had tonsilitis and I could not talk or swallow when I left the trenches and since I left the trenches I have developed a kind of rheumatism in my foot from always having cold feet and wet boots and socks. My throat has quite dissapeared [sic] now however and my foot is much better so that I hope to be out of hospital by next Wednesday. Today is Saturday. I have also been inoculated since I have been here for enteric. This is a queer little French town. I cannot name it but we are very comfortable here. There are 8 other officers from different regiments none of them are bad not even as bad as I am.

I want to get back to the front very badly as things seem to be livening up again. I don't know if it is only for the Kaiser's birthday. I think it is because the ground must be getting harder. I expect that they will keep me for a day or so at the base it is a way they have. If I have not stopped a bullet I shall be getting leave in two months time. I hope I may go over and see you all.

I have had no letters for 14 days now partly because I have been here for 8 days and because we were on the move before that, so there will be plenty for me to answer when I get back. Can you please tell Auntie Louise [another of his father's sisters] *that a cake is a thing that we never get out here? I wonder if she could send me one as in the trenches we only get the same food as the men and sometimes not enough of that.*

I will write again soon and send you something I have kept as a surprise.

Ever yours,

Jack.

He returned to duty with his regiment on 19 February 1915.

Morale remained high in the Patricias, despite the steady barrage of shells and bombs and the toll taken by German snipers. Colonel Farquhar retaliated by establishing his own sniping section under a Lt Colquhoun, which in one two day period accounted for seventeen of the enemy. The Colonel also introduced the practice of 'reconnaissance in force', which became known as trench raids and were adopted throughout the Canadian Corps. The first of these raids was brilliantly successful and congratulations were received from Brigade, Division, Corps and Army Commanders, even from the Commander in Chief himself.

Retaliation was not long in coming and in two days the regiment suffered over 70 casualties.

On 2 March Minchin wrote again to his grandfather:

My dear GP,

I wrote about 14 days ago and yesterday the letter was returned to me. It has apparently been opened by the Censor who disapproved of its contents, as if I wasn't a much better judge than he was of what is information and what isn't. All he does is to sit in an office and grow fat while we do the work. Considering it might have been my last letter it is d...... inconsiderate of him.

We have actually been doing some fighting lately. There are some extremely warm corners round this part of the world. I am getting heartily sick of life in the trenches. It is not what it is cracked up to be. And seeing people you have known well for some time being killed one after the other does not tend to brighten one's spirits up. We have lost about a third of our officers roughly.

I had a short letter from Harry and I have had some 300 cigarettes and 4 lbs of tobacco from you for which I thank you very much indeed. I am going into the trenches again tomorrow to harry the Germans and I expect they will come in most useful then.

This country will be positively terrible in the summer. We had to bury a man in the trench the other day as the stretcher bearers were too busy with the wounded and in digging a hole about 3 feet deep we came across the remains of 3 other dead men, and when the weather gets warm you can imagine how these will blend? in the summer sun.

There is really very little news here. If I tell you anything about the fracas we had a few days ago the confounded censor will probably stop it so I shall have to wait until I go over. We have been out quite a long time now. I think it is time we get some leave but I doubt if we shall yet as things are getting busier.

A very amusing thing happened the other day. The subaltern in the next trench to me was being bombed by the Germans in front of him, and he threw back a bomb for every one they threw at him until he ran out of them and then in desperation he threw back a tin of Ticklers Plum and Apple jam hoping that the Germans would think it was a bomb. You can imagine their consternation when the thing did not burst.

Things look pretty bright about the war now. I hope it won't last as long as we at first thought it would.

I must end now. I am writing to Aunt Georgie and Aunt Minnie.

Yours ever,

Jack.

Little did he know it but his trench war was almost over. In the weeks until 23 March, the regiment had suffered 238 battle casualties in addition to losses from sickness. Only ten of the twenty-seven officers were left, and the ten included Minchin. The order for his transfer to the Royal Flying Corps came through at last and on 11 March he reported to RFC HQ at St Omer, soon to be transferred to 1 Squadron.

Grandfather Minchin must have written to the Patricias' commanding officer to enquire after his grandson, for he next received a letter from

Captain HC Buller, formerly Adjutant, and temporarily commanding the regiment following the death of Colonel Farquhar on the very night, 19/20 March, on which the battalion was relieved. Major Hamilton Gault had already been wounded carrying an injured man across open ground in front of the Patricias' trenches. Captain Buller's letter read as follows:

March 30th.

Dear Sir,

I received your letter of March 17th. Lieutenant Minchin has left the Regiment and gone to join the Flying Corps and was to have reported at St Omer a fortnight ago. I havn't heard from him since he left. We were all very sorry to lose him as he was very popular in the Battalion and invaluable to it as a splendid and most efficient officer.

Yours sincerely,

H.C. Buller[8], Captain,
Commdg. P.P.C.L.I.

---

[9] Buller was later to command the regiment as Lt Colonel and to lose his life at Sanctuary Wood in June 1916.

Chapter Six

1 Squadron

Minchin was now attached to the Royal Flying Corps as a probationary observer, based at St Omer, although it would be some six months before his appointment to the RFC was gazetted. He wrote from St Omer on 22 March 1915:

My dear old GP,

Thank you ever so much for your letter. I meant to keep this as a surprise but apparently you have forstalled me. I am at present attached to the Royal Flying Corps as an observer, but I hope to get into it properly in a few months. I am at present attached to them on probation for a month but I think they will keep me. I have so far passed any task they have put on me. I have had some very exciting times. I went out one day with a pilot and in a snowstorm. We flew at 5000 for some time, then lost our way and had to come down to 50 feet to see the ground. We came down just over the German lines and they blazed away at us for about a minute and we escaped with only a few bullet holes in the machine. I expect they find it rather hard to hit us going down wind at about 100 miles an hour in the blinding sleet and snow.

This is much better than the trenches, not so depressing and not nearly so dangerous. When you are flying high they try and hit you with aeroplane guns but they never burst nearer than 3 or 4 hundred feet. I am fairly busy here and we have to get up quite early in the morning. But we are a long way behind the firing line. By the way don't put the name of the town on the envelope you send me, I believe we may be moving soon. Just put the RFC Expeditionary Force.

I must end now. Thank you ever so much for sending me the parcels. I have not got them. I only got one from Aunt Georgie yesterday.

Yours ever,

Jack

Lts M McB Bell-Irving, EO Grenfell and FF Minchin with a Caudron G3
(Bailleul Asylum in the background).

The date of this letter suggests that his attachment to 1 Squadron was immediate. The squadron had moved from Netheravon to St Omer on 7 March as a reconnaissance unit and began operations under the command of Major Geoffrey Salmond[10] on 10 March. In the RFC there was no systematic training of observers at this time, almost all candidates receiving on-the-job training in squadrons. This included map-reading, artillery observation (known as art. obs.) and general reconnaissance, including photographic. Minchin's service record states that he was graded a 'qualified observer' on 20 March 1915, a mere nine days after his transfer to the RFC.

As the war progressed, and fighting in the air intensified, the observer operated increasingly in the role of air gunner. Navigation remained largely in the hands of the pilot. However it was a route onto a pilot's course and many famous aces such as McCudden, Bishop and Ira Jones began their flying lives as observers. In these early days, Minchin would have been spared participation in the vicious air battles that came during

[10] Later Air Chief Marshal Sir Geoffrey Salmond, KCB, KCMG, DSO

the summer and autumn of 1915. As an observer in the early months of 1915, he would have been able to perform his reconnaissance tasks in daylight and without serious interference by the enemy.

The squadron had arrived in France on 8 March, equipped with four BE8s, a Caudron G3, a Bristol Scout D and eight Avro 504s. Their arrival coincided with the battle of Neuve Chapelle and the squadron flew its first reconnaissance within 48 hours of arriving. On 12 March the first offensive sortie was flown. Four aircraft attempted to destroy a rail bridge near Douai and a railway junction at Don with 20lb bombs dropped over the side by pilots, because observers were not being carried. On 29 March, the squadron moved to Bailleul as a part of the 2nd Wing in support of II Corps, just eleven miles west of the front line at Ypres, where it remained for three years. It was a pleasant aerodrome, and some personnel were accommodated initially – some wags said appropriately – in a large lunatic asylum on the edge of the airfield.

Minchin was kept busy during his five months with 1 Squadron. During April, tunnels were being dug and mines laid preparatory to a major assault on 17 April on Hill 60, a small hill to the south of Zillebeke used by the Germans to observe British positions around Ypres. The squadron had the task of keeping the sky above the area clear of German reconnaissance machines. From 16 April the front from Kemmel to Ypres was patrolled from 0430 until 1915 hours. Thanks very largely to this work, the attack on Hill 60 took the enemy completely by surprise. On 18 April the squadron made their first claim for the downing of an enemy machine. By the end of April, they were flying a mixed bag of aircraft: three Avro 504s, four Morane Parasols, one Martinsyde S1 and a single remaining BE8. In the period up to 20 June, the squadron also flew 141 bombing sorties against railway junctions and bridges behind enemy lines, although bombing, at this stage in the war, was, to say the least, an inexact science. There was no form of sighting apparatus and bombs were dropped more or less haphazardly over the side by the observer with few tangible results.

Early in the summer of 1915 the Germans introduced the first aircraft specifically designed for aerial combat, the Fokker E1 *Eindecker*, with synchronized Parabellum machine guns firing through the propeller. Although the enemy scouts rarely ventured across Allied lines, they caused heavy losses to the RFC two-seater squadrons, to the extent that the period became known as the 'Fokker Scourge'.

On 6 July the squadron suffered its first fatal casualty. Lt Lambert Playfair, who had joined the squadron in March a few days before Minchin and who, like Minchin, had learned to fly at the Eastbourne aerodrome, lost his life while flying as an observer on an artillery observation patrol over St Julien.

Minchin's civilian flying licence was not recognized by the RFC and, after flying as an observer for some five eventful months with 1 Squadron, he was on 5 August posted to 23 Squadron in England and thence to the Central Flying School, attached to 1 Reserve Squadron at Farnborough. By 5 October he had qualified as a pilot to the RFC's standards and was promoted lieutenant on 1 November. He was then re-appointed to 23 Squadron as a preliminary to his transfer to 14 Squadron which had been forming up at Shoreham airfield since 3 February 1915, preparatory to its embarkation for service in Egypt.

Chapter Seven

14 Squadron

The fourteen months that Minchin spent with 14 Squadron in North Africa proved to be some of the most successful of his whole combat flying career. He was just 25, had survived the horrors of trench warfare in Flanders and had cut his flying teeth with 1 Squadron in France. Furthermore he would be serving in an environment which gave his undoubted courage and skill as a pilot full rein, with few of the distractions and temptations to which he was so prone to succumb. During this period, which included a month's home leave, he was awarded the Military Cross and Bar and was twice mentioned in despatches. Fortuitously, Egypt was at this time an area of operation which, although incurring pilot casualties, did not suffer them at anything like the appalling level that was being experienced on the Western Front. One reason was that the enemy had nothing comparable to the highly effective AA batteries that the Germans deployed on the Western Front. Fortunately also, these

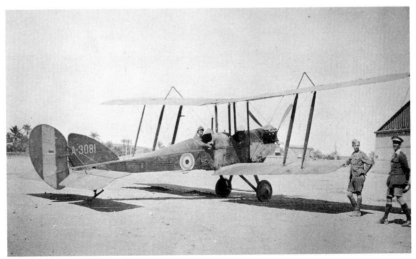

A BE2c

Minchin with 14 Squadron   Flypast in the desert. Minchin in the leading aircraft

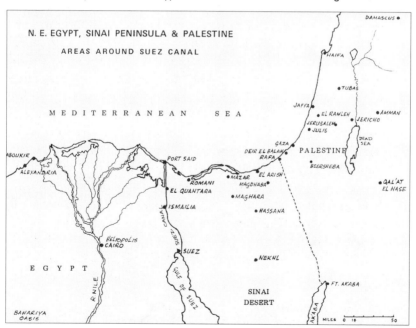

Sinai

Minchin on the further camel

fourteen months are exceedingly well documented, the files[11] containing several reports written by Minchin following his solo reconnaissances, although when an observer was carried, it was he who would write the report.

The squadron had been formed at Shoreham in Sussex in February 1915 with an assortment of aircraft, predominantly BE2cs. It soon moved to Hounslow Heath and then to Gosport, which is where Lt Minchin joined it as a CFS trained pilot on 27 October. By this time the squadron's aircraft included 21 BE2cs, five Martinsyde S1s, three Caudrons, four Farman S11 Shorthorns, four Blériots and sundry other machines. Within ten days, on 7 November 1915, the squadron, under the command of Major GE Todd, set sail from Avonmouth in the Australian Blue Funnel liner *SS Anchises* as a part of 5 Wing, RFC. Some of the aircraft, certainly the BE2cs, were crated and sailed with them. Their Wing Commander, Lt Col Geoffrey Salmond, later to succeed Trenchard as Commander of the RFC in the Field, travelled overland via Marseilles. Salmond had been Minchin's commanding officer with 1 Squadron in France in 1915.

On 17 November 1915 they arrived at Alexandria and within a few days had established the squadron at Ismailia[12] , a small town on Lake

---

[11] To be found at the National Archives under AIR 1 1661, 1752–3, 1755–6

[12] Ismailia was a small French-influenced town that had been founded by Ferdinand de Lesseps as a base camp while building the Suez Canal.

At Alexandria

Timsa, at the southern end of the Suez Canal. Captain JC Watson[13], the squadron's first historian, later wrote of Ismailia: *an oasis of shade and tropical luxuriance in striking contrast with the hard glaring desert that surrounds it, designed and laid out with that happy symmetry in which the French excel, fated to be all that most of the squadron were to see of civilisation for many a day.* Almost at once the three flights were dispersed to landing grounds at Mersah Matruh, Sinai and Kantara. This was a direct consequence of the vast area, the Sinai Peninsula, that the Wing was responsible for and would continue to be throughout Minchin's service with the squadron and indeed beyond. Sinai was a huge triangular waste of shifting sand, crossed by three main routes which met at El Arish. Sandstorms were a perennial problem and would prevent flying, sometimes for days. Throughout 1916, the RFC pilots carried out innumerable long flights over this featureless country where the environment was naturally hostile and the Arabs were a formidable enemy.

Minchin would soon find himself at Kantara with 'C' Flight, only 30 miles from the Turkish lines.

[13] Later Sir John Charles Watson MBE KC LLB

Meanwhile though, he was relaxing at the Grand Hotel at Alexandria, from where on 9 December he wrote to his grandfather in Ireland:

Machines are being unloaded. Bored; playing golf, tennis and croquet. The other two flights are all over Egypt with old machines which another Sqn left behind. 'C' Flight [his] are going to take the new machines. It is very slack here compared to France. It is very cosmopolitan, every nation under the sun, mostly French and Greeks with a lot of Italians, Arabs, Senussi, Armenians and not many English, who are nearly all at Cairo.

The squadron's role was to act as the eyes of the army in the campaign in Sinai, Arabia and Palestine, in the defence of the Suez Canal, against Turkish, German and German-led Senussi forces under the command of the German General Liman von Sanders. They were to engage in reconnaissance, photo-reconnaissance and, occasionally, bombing raids against enemy troops, aerodromes and water supplies; all this on an almost daily basis.

The desert climate soon began to cause problems. Tented accommodation for all ranks proved hard to adapt to after more temperate northern climes. Water would always be chronically short. Extreme heat during the day and freezing temperatures at night played havoc with the aircrafts' wood, fabric and engines, to the extent that the Wing ordered that the floors and walls of all hangars should if possible be sprinkled with water three times a day. In flight, water-cooled engines boiled away their water and over-heated oil soon lost its lubricating qualities. Extra radiators and oil tanks had to be improvised. Forced landings in the desert were everyday hazards and all aircraft were required to carry four days' food and water, a rifle, a signal pistol, smoke bombs and strips of cloth to lay out in the sand. Gold coins were sewn into clothing as an inducement to Arabs to rescue them.

Minchin's first operational flight took place on 3 January 1916. It was an early morning photo reconnaissance from Ismailia in a BE2c with a Lt HV Stammers[14] as his observer. It ended in near disaster. After taking their photos, they were forced to land at Romani, some distance on the wrong side of the Canal, probably due to engine trouble. They decided

---

[14] Later CO of 15 Squadron in France.

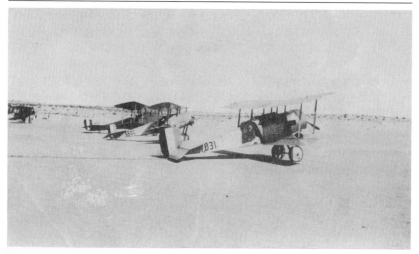

The aerodrome at Ismailia

to destroy their camera and, taking the camera's lens and the exposed plates with them, walked the 21 miles back to Kantara. The aircraft was later recovered.

In the months through to June, 'C' Flight carried out daily reconnaissances and Minchin regularly flew on them with a variety of observers, there being no attempt to develop pilot/observer pairings. This may have been because several of the observers were Army officers attached to the RFC for training and liaison duties. After all, the squadron's primary purpose was to act as the eyes of the soldiers on the ground. But the squadron's operations were also offensive. The governing factor in all land-based operations in the Sinai Peninsula was the water supply. The Turkish line of defence consisted of a series of battalion-strength posts round the water holes. Consequently Turkish defensive positions, oases and their water supplies were bombed, though the bombing was primitive in the extreme. Most of the bombs were small, 20lbs, with the occasional 100lb one thrown in for good measure. Bomb racks were mounted under each wing and under the centre fuselage and these could carry either 4 x 20lb or 1 x 100lb bombs. Later the 'C' Flight commander designed and built a bomb sight from wood, string and a spirit level.

On 8 February, Minchin wrote again to his grandfather; this time from Kantara:

I looped the loop for the first time the other day. It was surprisingly easy. Saw Harry on the station at Ismailia. We can live on very little – I hope to put by about 1£ a day for a time.

Was the usually profligate Minchin indeed able to save some £300 by the time that his tour of duty in Egypt came to an end?

The squadron's primitive BE2cs[15] were adequate when the enemy was on the ground and equipped only with rifles and, occasionally, anti-aircraft guns. The arrival in March of the German air unit, Flieger Abteilung 300, based at Beersheba and equipped with 14 Rumpler C1s and two Pfalz EIIs, brought a new dimension to the war for 14 Squadron, although there were to be surprisingly few occasions when the two forces clashed in the air. It was not until May that the first BE2c was shot down by an enemy aircraft and it was in August that the squadron was able to claim its first kill.

In April Geoffrey Salmond, promoted Brig Gen RFC, took command of the Middle East Brigade and Lt Col Philip Joubert de la Ferté, who had commanded 1 Squadron in France just after Minchin's transfer to CFS, assumed command of 5 Wing on 1 July. Joubert was to serve with distinction through the post-war years and World War Two. His view of the conditions surrounding his new command was despondent, as recorded in his 1952 autobiography[16]:

The 5th Wing's resources were not large, and our equipment was markedly inferior to that of the enemy. The Turks, having no air force worth mentioning, relied entirely on their German allies for air support. Our old BEs and FEs, mounting at most a couple of hand-held Lewis guns, were faced by Aviatiks, superior in performance and with two machine guns firing through the propeller. On form, therefore, the RFC should have been shot out of the sky in the air battle that accompanied the Turkish advance overland. We did indeed suffer relatively heavy casualties, but the Germans' technical superiority was not matched by the quality of their pilots. So we managed to hold our own during the early stages of the fighting, and when the land battle turned to our advantage and the Turks were chased home across the Sinai Peninsula, we had good hunting against both air and land targets.

[15] Maximum speed 72mph, altitude 10,000 feet.
[16] *The Fated Sky* by Sir Philip Joubert de la Ferté (Hutchinson 1952).

Minchin standing left, with 14 Squadron officers

With a squadron pet or mascot, possibly a bear cub

Minchin seems to have been particularly effective in locating enemy concentrations and then in leading bombing raids against them. For example, on 23 April the British ground forces had been ejected from their positions at Katia[17] by the Turks. Minchin located 1000 of the enemy there on the evening of 23 April and the following morning he led eight aircraft at 2000 feet for the forty minute flight, arriving at 0555 hrs. Once there he dropped a smoke ball as a signal to start the attack and, diving towards the target, released his bombs from 700 feet. The rest of the formation followed him down and in all seventy bombs were dropped. Six of the aircraft then descended to 200 feet and strafed the enemy positions with machine guns. The remaining two pilots flew further east looking for more Turks and found a body of some 1000 at Bir el-Abd which they also attacked with machine gun fire. The next day eight aircraft attacked the Bir el-Abd positions again but were themselves attacked by an enemy aeroplane. One BE2c was damaged and Lt CR Rowden was wounded in the knee. However all the aircraft returned safely and, after rearming, four aircraft left Kantara to attack Bir el-Abd again. In all, nine separate attacks were made by the RFC against the Turkish forces over the three days, 23, 24 and 25 April, before the Turks finally withdrew. These exploits were recognized specifically when his Military Cross was gazetted on 31 May with the following citation:

For conspicuous gallantry and skill on many occasions, notably when leading a successful bomb and machine gun raid on a force of the enemy which he had located overnight. Next day he took part in two other raids. During these operations he flew for 13 hours over enemy country.

On 1 May 1916 Minchin's much-loved grandfather, 'GP', died. Apart from his brother Harry, his grandfather was the only member of his family with whom he had a significant emotional link. Falkiner John had provided a firm and indeed stabilizing foundation for Minchin through the turmoils of his early manhood, and his influence would be sorely missed by his grandson in the years to come.

The German unit at El-Arish had made several bombing raids on Port Said and so, in retaliation, on 18 May the squadron mounted a combined attack on El-Arish aerodrome. Three aircraft joined with

---

[17] Also known as Qatiya.

three machines from the Royal Naval Air Service (RNAS) seaplane carrier *Ben-my-Chree*, commanded by the redoubtable Commander C R Samson, who piloted a Short seaplane. Forty bombs were dropped and shells were fired from the three naval vessels.

On 13 June Minchin reconnoitred El-Arish airfield, dropping a bomb on what was now the base of the German Flieger Abteilung 300. This was the precursor to a major attempt to eliminate the German aircraft on the ground, because of the threat they posed to the virtually defenceless BE2cs. Five days later Minchin led a substantial attack on the airfield with no fewer than eleven aircraft, eight from 14 Squadron supplemented by a further three from 17 Squadron. Two BEs, each carrying an observer, flew over El-Arish at 7000ft to protect the other nine, which were all flown as single seaters to increase the bomb load. Two of the BEs, including Minchin's, carried 100lb blockbusters. The first, flown by 2Lt ASC MacLaren, dropped its bomb from 100 feet, destroying an enemy aircraft and its personnel on the ground. Two more German machines were hit, as were six of the ten hangars. Once they had dropped their bombs, the BEs strafed the aerodrome with machine gun fire. Three BE2cs were lost, though two crews were rescued – apart from Capt RJ Tipton[18], who became a prisoner of war. Minchin left a handwritten report of his role in this daring action. In fact he had been appointed Flight Commander with the rank of temporary captain on 15 June.

About this time the squadron was issued with some new aircraft to supplement the slow and vulnerable BE2cs: five Martinsyde G100 Elephants and six Airco de Havilland DH1s, two-seater pushers with 120hp Beardmore engines and a single Lewis gun on a flexible pillar mounted in the front cockpit. The Martinsydes, large single-seat scouts with a top speed of 103mph, were the fastest machines yet used by the RFC in the Middle East and, as a sturdy weight-lifter, could operate as both a bomber and fighter. The de Havillands were deemed to be of limited use as escort-fighters. There were also two 'useless' Curtiss JN-3s, machines that were essentially trainers.

Minchin continued to fly meticulously observed reconnaissance sorties. On 6 July, flying a BE2c solo, he visited El-Kharari, Bir el-Melhi,

---

[18] Tipton escaped and received a MiD for his service while in captivity. Serving with 40 Squadron in France, he was wounded in action and died on 12 March 1918.

Report on Bomb Dropping at El Arish

June 18th 1916.

I arrived at the Aerodrome at El Arish at 8.10. when I got there there was a machine just in front of one of the sheds (a) turning, I dropped a 100 lb bomb on the camp from 700 feet on the altimetre, which did not explode, I then turned to the right and dropped two 20 lb bombs on the wooden sheds, during the whole of this time there was considerable rifle fire, so I climbed to 1500 doing one circuit of the aerodrome. On coming round I saw a new German biplane, with large Iron crosses on the wing tips, in the wadi south of the sheds, there was no one in it, so I dropped the last two bombs on it, one going within 20 feet, just as I left a second machine bombed it, 8 bombs falling within 50 yards of it. When I left at 8.35 the aerodrome & sheds seemed to have suffered severely. On the way home a machine fired two smoke balls, and landed in the sea, near a motor boat, he was picked up.

F. F. Minchin Lt RFC.

Minchin's report of the bombing of El-Arish airfield.

With a two-seater DH1a

Bir el-Maghara and El-Baiga and dropped a 100lb bomb on an enemy camp, reporting 'no apparent damage'. Then, on 11 July, he departed for a well deserved four-week leave in England.

While he was away, the British army on 5 August crushed a Turkish offensive around Romani and Bir el-Mazar; 4000 prisoners were taken and the last Turkish threat to the Suez Canal was averted. The squadron was deeply involved and aircrew carried out two or three sorties each day in support of the ground troops.

On 30 August Minchin carried out his first photo-reconnaissance since returning from leave, flying a BE2c with 2Lt HJ Buchanan-Wollaston[19] as observer. Leaving Ismailia at 0510, they reported significant quantities of tents and camels at Maghara. Two days later, on 1 September, Minchin led an eight aircraft bombing raid on the camps and water tank at Maghara. During the action Lt ASC MacLaren force-landed and Minchin landed to pick him up, unfortunately damaging his own undercarriage. After the damaged machines had

---

[19] HJ Buchanan-Wollaston had joined 14 Squadron as Recording Officer (ie adjutant) on 31 July 1916 and qualified as an observer on 3 September. From 18 August 1917 until 4 February 1918 he served as a pilot.

been burned, the two pilots were picked up by Lts HA Fordham and WJY Guilfoyle[20].

Then on 4 and 6 September, he flew from Mahemdia aerodrome what were described as 'protective reconnaissances' over Ismailia. In fact his reconnaissances were aggressive as well as protective, as his 6 September report reveals:

Report on bomb raid on El Arish.

I left Mahemdia Aerodrome at 7am with eight bombs. On arriving at GALSS the de Havilland, which was acting as an escort, had a forced landing. I saw it go down and went on to El Arish where I arrived at 8.20.

I then photographed from the Southern Camp at El Arish to the Aerodrome, and when I had taken 4, I was attacked at fairly long range by an enemy aeroplane. I finished the photographing and being over the aerodrome I proceeded to drop my bombs. Two fell to the north of the Aerodrome Camp, the nearest about 50 yards off. The next three fell just East of the Western three hangars, fairly close. By this time the German machine was close up, so I turned quickly back towards the Aerodrome, dropping my last three bombs and made off towards the sea. The German was then firing on my tail, and I could see explosions from my last three bombs.

On the way home (30 miles west of El Arish), the enemy machine overtook the other BE2c [Lt Fordham], *but retreated after exchanging fire with it when he saw my machine going to go into the fight.*

The de Havilland at GALSS had out a K [a signal: Message Received] *so I went to MAHEMDIA.*

Signed

FF Minchin, Capt.
Sept. 6th 1916
Ismailia

After three more solo reconnaissances, Minchin, flying from Mahemdia at 0245, took part in another successful bombing raid on El Arish aerodrome:

---

[20] Later Air Commodore RAF, OBE, MC

REPORT ON BOMBING RAID ON EL ARISH

I left the Aerodrome at Mahemdia at 2.45pm [should be am] *and following the sea coast reached the WADI EL ARISH at about 4am. I then turned South and when I was over EL ARISH town, I saw bombs exploding on the aerodrome. I could not see the result, but when I got there the smoke was still distinguishable among the hangars. I then went over the line of sheds allotted to me, dropping one bomb on each shed as I passed over. I hit the second shed from the North, I then dropped my last two bombs on the Aerodrome Camp, there was a row of bivouacks, and two larger tents or sheds. One bomb fell right in the middle.*

The stillness of the air and the low altitude resulted in the bombing being more accurate than in any of my raids previously.

I noticed both going and returning a semicircle of 4 fires about a mile apart running roughly North and South about on the line GERERAT to EL MASHALFAT about 8 miles west of EL ARISH. They seemed to be the fires of an outpost line.

I landed on the MAHEMDIA AERODROME again at about 5.50am.

Signed FF Minchin
Captain RFC

On 18 September, he flew with Capt Macaulay to locate a wrecked aircraft. Frequent reconnaissances followed until, on 25 September, Minchin's first mention in despatches was gazetted. Three days later, flying a Martinsyde and accompanied by Lts RP Willock[21] and ER Cottier in a de Havilland, they engaged an Aviatik over El-Arish. The Aviatik, with two machine guns firing through the propeller, was a formidable foe although on this occasion there was no blood lost on either side.

On 5 October Minchin flew solo in a Martinsyde to recce Mahemdia and El-Arish. His report reads:

The camp just south of the town [presumably El Arish] *was the same as in the photographs. There was a small scattered camp about*

---

[21] Later Air Vice Marshal RP Willock CB.

12 tents west of the town. The trenches on the sea coast have been extended; at each end there is a redoubt. Just east of the town there are a few scattered tents. The main camp is south east of the town, and consists of 7 large and about 25 to 30 small tents; also 14 brown shelters. The Aerodrome is evacuated. There seemed to be very little movement about the town. The roads south are heavily marked.

1000 Landed.
Clouds obstructed observation on way home.

Signed F.F. Minchin Capt.

After two more accompanied reconnaissances on 10 and 13 October, he was aloft again on 15 October, solo in a Martinsyde, this time for five hours, with a one and a half hour break to load more bombs. His objective was to attack and support the capture of Maghara Camp and to destroy its water supply. His report reads as follows:

0830	*Maghara: Camp as before, no movements. I dropped 2 bombs on the BARGA ROAD near point 1841 and 1 near the Northern Camp.*
0840	*Werib: All clear.*
0845	*Hamma: Camp as before, no movements, dropped 1 bomb.*
0855	*Meneidret El Litheili: The road was clear to HASSANA. Dropped message to RAKWA.*
0930–1100	*Salmana: Landed. Got more bombs.*
1120–1200	*Maghara: Could see no sign of troops on Eastern Flank except horses held North of Wadi SAFAAT. Main attack appeared to be in front of trenches near 1211. Dropped my bombs on MAGHARA CAMP. Engaged about 40 camels and flock of goats retreating to WERIB with machine gun. On opening fire on the trench near 1211 with machine gun I had a jamb and returned home.*

Signed F. Minchin Capt.

That he was entrusted with this arduous mission without escort demonstrates the confidence that his commanding officer reposed in him at this time.

The London Gazette on 25 November 1916 recorded the award of a Bar to Minchin's Military Cross with the citation:

> *For conspicuous gallantry in action. He flew 150 miles at night to bomb an enemy aerodrome, descending to 500 feet and doing serious damage. On another occasion he landed 45 miles from our line to pick up the pilot of a damaged machine in hostile country.*

A week later, on 2 December, Minchin was attacked by two Fokkers and an Aviatik while over Gaza and Beersheba. His fuel tank was hit and he force-landed near Rafah, east of the lines. After burning his aircraft, he was rescued by Capt R H Freeman[22] who drove off the enemy aircraft. Minchin rode back perched astride the cowl of Freeman's Martinsyde, the pursuing enemy no more than 200 yards away.

On 22 December, 14 Squadron moved forward to establish a new aerodrome at Mustabig, a large, flat salt pan half way across Sinai and just south of the Bardawil Peninsula. This reduced significantly the long distances that had to be flown before making contact with the enemy. Working with the Army, this provided a base from which to launch a successful assault on El-Arish. The village and water holes were taken and the Turks withdrew eastwards towards Beersheba.

The Turks left a detachment of 500 men at a waterhole called Maghdaba, about 70 miles north of El-Arish. 14 Squadron, in cooperation with 67 (Australian) Squadron, later re-designated as 1 Squadron, Australian Flying Corps, dropped 126 bombs on the large Turkish camp at Magdhaba and machine-gunned the Turkish trenches, causing heavy damage. The Army then finished off the attack and the Turkish garrison surrendered.

As December approached its end, Minchin's second 'Mention' was gazetted and he received his posting to the Salonika front. With it came promotion to temporary major in command of 47 Squadron with effect from 1 January 1917.

---

[22] Major RH Freeman MC, C de G, MiD, later CO of 73 Squadron, was killed in action in France on 21 July 1918. His brother was Air Chief Marshal Sir Wilfred Freeman.

Chapter Eight

47 Squadron

Major Minchin

Minchin spent 15 months in command of 47 Squadron in Macedonia, the whole of 1917 and the first three months of 1918. The squadron formed a part of the Allied forces (British, French and Serbian) which were sent to assist Serbia when it was threatened by the Bulgarian and Austro-Hungarian armies in 1916. By early 1916, there were 300,000 Allied troops on a 90-mile front running up the Struma valley from the sea, across the shore of Lake Dojran to the Vardar River. The Bulgarian positions were strong, a chain of fortified strongholds in often mountainous terrain.

The squadron, together with 17 Squadron, formed 16 Wing RFC, commanded by Lt Col GWP Dawes. With 2 Wing RNAS based on the island of Thasos, it constituted the British air presence in the campaign. 17 Squadron had been transferred from Egypt, while 47 was a relatively new unit, having formed up at Beverley in March 1916. The squadron arrived at Salonika on 20 September 1916 and was soon based at Mikra Bay to operate in support of the Army XII Corps. 17 Squadron, with No 17 Kite Balloon Section, supported XVI Corps. The enemy air presence was almost entirely German.

The main work of 47 Squadron was to be photo reconnaissance and artillery spotting, with occasional bombing missions. Initially there was little fighting which was perhaps just as well, as their aircraft were at first obsolete BE2cs and AW FK3s[23]. The latter were sometimes pressed into service as bombers, with the BE2cs forming their escorts.

The climate proved to be a major hazard. During the winter months they experienced snow, freezing weather and heavy rain leading to ankle-deep mud. The summers in contrast were hot, humid, fetid and fly and mosquito-ridden. They had few fresh foodstuffs and sanitation was poor. Unsurprisingly there was much disease: dysentry, typhoid, malaria[24], hepatitis, hypothermia and dehydration.

On 23 December 1916 the squadron's first commanding officer, Major Cyril Wigram, was posted back to England, suffering from dysentry. On the same day, 23 December, the squadron registered its first kill. Capt WDM Bell, an elephant hunter well-known in East Africa as 'Karamoja' Bell, flying a BE12, shot down an enemy 2-seater north of Selimli. On the same day two FK3s destroyed an enemy aircraft over Hudova. Typical of the extraordinary chivalry exhibited by both airforces in this campaign, on Christmas Day greetings and a message of condolence for Bell's victim were dropped on the German aerodrome at Hudova.

Minchin arrived on the 1 January 1917 and the squadron's three flights were dispersed to separate airfields at Janes and Snevce. Soon after landing at Janes, the squadron adopted a young crane which had crashed onto the airstrip with a broken wing. Christened 'Charles Mascot', it died in July 1917 despite intensive nursing. It did though provide the centerpiece for the squadron's badge, 'a demoiselle crane'.

---

[23] Armstrong Whitworth FK3s were referred to as 'Little Acks' (and AW FK8s as 'Big Acks'). This was the only theatre in which the FK3 served operationally.

[24] Malaria was the biggest cause of casualties in Salonika. The journal of the Salonika Veterans' Association was known as *The Mosquito*.

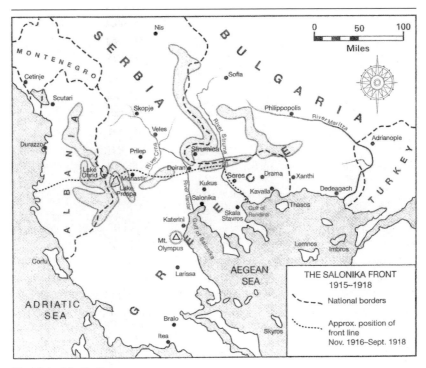

Map of the Salonika Front

On 5 January eight 47 Squadron aircraft led by Capt Alan Goodfellow bombed Hudova station, one FK3 being downed by anti-aircraft fire, the pilot Lt AND Pocock being made a PoW. Ten days later another FK3 was shot down at Smolari near Lake Dojran while escorting a reconnaissance patrol. The Germans later dropped a note (and bombs) notifying the RFC of the deaths of the crew (2Lts SJM White and H Matthews):

The Royal Flying Corps.

The German aviators are very sorry to inform you of the death of the two English aviators which were killed on the 15th January 10.30 am, after a fight with our aeroplanes. The English aviators had been fighting very bravely, but their aeroplane dropped after about 5 minutes fight and 'skilled.' They died as heroes, and have all our respects. Their bodies will be buried with all military honours.

   We are informing you also of your lieutenant Pocock having been made prisoner by the troops without being blessed [wounded].

*We are obliged of your having informed us of the four German
aviators which have been made your prisoners.*

'The German Flying Corps'

So the year continued. Although we have a history of the squadron's life
during this period (*Over the Balkans and South Russia, 1923*), written
by one of Minchin's 47 Squadron officers, Lt HA Jones[25], he makes no
mention of Minchin apart from noting his arrival and departure, even
though he includes any amount of operational detail and of the men
and machines involved.

The squadron continued to support the troops on the ground, despite
knee-deep mud and snow which 'turned landing strips into impassable
black glue, rotted wooden aircraft frames, soaked canvas, congealed oil,
jammed guns and split rubber.'

On 26 February, the enemy brought a group of 20 aircraft (Kampf-
geschwader 1) from Bucharest where it had been employed against the
Rumanians and Russians following distinguished service on the Western
Front. Jones waxes eloquent:

*Like a bolt from the blue they first appeared on February the 26th.
Twenty machines, flying fairly low and in superb formation . . . As
the machines came nearer they lost their aspect of wild duck and
looked, to quote one observer, like cathedrals flying through the air.*

Well practised in formation bombing, the unit was equipped with
powerful, modern machines: Halberstadts with 120hp Mercedes engines,

---

[25] In August 1917 Jones was severely wounded in an action for which he received the MC and the French
Croix de Guerre. Piloted by Lt F W H Thomas, another big game hunter, this time from Rhodesia, in
an FK8 on a DPA (Deep Penetration Attack) on the Bulgarian Army HQ at Prilep, Thomas was hit in
the back while Jones was wounded in the mouth, stomach and left hand. Thomas, barely conscious,
nursed the machine some 20 miles back to base where he insisted on dictating his report before
receiving medical attention. He died 4½ months later in hospital in England. Jones was later to author
volumes 2 to 6 of the official history of the air war: *The War in the Air* (Oxford University Press, 1928).
It is unbelievable that Minchin would not have played a part in the squadron's activities in the air, so
it has to be assumed that the personalities of the two men clashed to the extent that Jones found it
possible to recount in some detail the squadron's operations without reference to its commanding
officer. Presumably though, Minchin was not involved in any action which involved losses to personnel
or aircraft, or Jones would have been obliged to mention it. There was also Trenchard's decree that
no commanding officer should fly east of the lines, though it is unlikely that Minchin would have
observed it. Sadly the squadron's operational records are not lodged at the National Archives and so
we are heavily dependent on Jones's record.

AEGs with 220hp Mercedes engines, Rumplers with two Benz engines and one Gotha, all of which were supported from a railway train. They began their campaign by bombing the French airfield at Gorgop, destroying eight aircraft and damaging four more. Jones states that the French were no longer able to continue patrolling their lines between the Vardar and Isvor and 47 Squadron was ordered to extend their patrolling in the direction of Gorgop. Before these orders reached 47, the same German group raided the British airfield at Janes. Most of 47's aircraft were able to get airborne in time but they were able only to watch as some 40 bombs burst around their hangars and tents. In the event, no great material damage was done although seven men were killed and Lt E McM Howes, the equipment officer, and eight men were wounded. The following day they came again, twenty aircraft flying like ducks or geese in V-shape formation. This time however their target was the British camp at Salonika. They were opposed by seven available machines from 17 Squadron and, despite the superior numbers, the formation was broken up and one Halberstadt scout forced to land, the pilot being taken prisoner. They bombed Salonika successfully however. Just north of the town was a base camp called Summerhill where 376 casualties were suffered. The 47 Squadron aircraft were in the air waiting to intercept the raiders and each machine fought some three or four of the enemy. Although they inflicted some damage, there were no losses on either side and the German aircraft withdrew when they tired of the fight.

During March three retaliatory raids in strength were carried out by 17 and 47 Squadrons against Hudova airfield and against Cestovo. The Germans retaliated on 12 March by bombing Vertekop, the Salonika-Monastir railway and the British No 29 General Hospital, where two English nurses were killed. In mid-March a composite unit, 'E' Squadron, comprising four RNAS Sopwith 1½ Strutters, three 17 Squadron BE12s and two 47 Squadron DH2s, reinforced by a RNAS bomber group known as 'F' Squadron, was assembled to try to drive out Kampfgeschwader1. Four of the enemy aircraft were brought down by AA fire or by Allied aircraft and for about a week from 29 April until 5 May enemy bases, dumps and their aerodrome at Hudova were heavily bombed. This activity was successful, for by 11 May the hangars at Hudova had been dismantled and KG1 withdrew from the region to return to Belgium, complete with train, to renew its attacks on England. As Jones says: 'A sigh of relief went up at its departure…because it meant a temporary cessation of the pyjama-clad run from tent or hut to a dug-out, or a precipitate dash for machines.'

In February, April and May the British 22nd, 26th and 60th Divisions of XII Corps attacked on the Petit Couronné across the Jumeaux Ravine. The squadron, augmented by some new aircraft, DH2s, provided intensive air support against the Bulgarians, well-entrenched in timbered dugouts and concrete machine gun emplacements. The 7th Oxford and Bucks Light Infantry and the 7th Berkshires fought their way right up the precipitous side of the Petit Couronné and finally took and held the trenches on the summit. Almost all their officers were killed or wounded and they had to withdraw the next day. Losses on the ground were alarmingly high with, according to some accounts, some 4000 casualties in the three actions.

Minchin's squadron continued its reconnaissance and artillery observation patrols through April and May in support of the land battle of Dojran. At different times during April, 2Lt WH Farrow and Lt FWH Thomas, the big game hunter, had downed enemy machines. At the end of the month Minchin received a congratulatory message from General Sir HFM Wilson, GOC of XII Corps, praising the work done by the squadron during May:

> The Corps Commander desires me to convey to you, and to the
> officers and other ranks under your command, his great appreciation
> of the zeal shown by all ranks and the good work performed during
> the operations carried out by the XII Corps during the past month.
> He realizes clearly the strain imposed, not only upon pilots and
> observers, but also upon other ranks of the Royal Flying Corps
> in carrying out their duties at high pressure during a period of
> operations, and he has read with interest the reports rendered of the
> various flights carried out during this period.

In June a number of Vickers FB19s arrived to augment the squadron's fighting strength. A contemporary record notes 'torrential rain storms, flies, gnats, sand-flies and mosquitoes in millions, plus snakes and extreme heat.'

During the month, three major bombing raids on the enemy camps and supply dumps were flown. These were seen to cause him to move trains out of stations and to retire and sub-divide supply dumps. Following a series of successful reconnaissance missions, another congratulatory message was received from the Corps Commander:

> *The Corps Commander has read the summary of work carried out by the scouts and patrols under your command yesterday, and is well satisfied with the work carried out during the recent trying weather. He wishes you to inform your Flight Commanders that he watches their work with interest, and is fully aware of the difficulties with which they have to contend. 20.7.17*

August saw a continuation of mass bombing raids on enemy camps and airfields in conjunction with 17 Squadron and RNAS Thasos. The squadron continued these aggressive operations through October and November, which ended with Minchin receiving his third 'Mention'. During an attack on Cestovo Dump on 29 October by five 47 Squadron machines, they were attacked by eight Albatros and Halberstadt scouts. After a gallant fight, one of the British pilots, 2Lt PD Montague in a single-seater BE12, was shot down. Montague was an unlikely warrior who delighted in wildlife and constructed a lute with which he would entertain his comrades with his repertoire of mediaeval ballads.

On 30 October a German aircraft flew low over the airfield, dropping a message which included the advice:

> *Read the following chapters of the book:*
> *BASIC COMBAT IN THE AIR:*
> *CH 2 para 1 to 6 and CH 4 para 10b.*

In layman's terms, the message was: 'always watch your tail.' Was this chivalry or black humour? Some month or two later the Bulgarians dropped a message on Janes aerodrome which, translated, read:

> *On 29th of October 1917, one of your comrades* [clearly Montague] *met with a hero's death in an air fight. He was buried with due honours and a memorial stone has been put up over his grave[26], but without an inscription, as his name is not known to us. In order that we may make good this deficiency, kindly inform us as to his name*

---

[26] His grave was lost and he is commemorated on the Dojran Memorial.

and the date and place of his birth. The reply should be addressed to the 'Bulgarian Airmen'.

November 21 saw an incident which, though not directly involving 47 Squadron, many in this gentlemanly air war found distasteful. A Lt von Eschwege, who had accounted for twenty Allied aircraft, was killed when attacking a decoy balloon from 17 Squadron Kite Balloon Section which was loaded with 500lbs of high explosive.

In December1917, there was yet another commendation from the Corps Commander, this time directed at the gunners and their RFC spotters, both observers and pilots:

To the General Officer Commanding, Royal Artillery:

The Corps Commander has instructed me to express through you, to the Batteries and the RFC observers concerned, his appreciation of the good work done during the past month in destructive shoots.

Batteries 13th, 18th, 186th, 190th and 201st Heavies, and 43rd, 130th, 138th Siege.

Observers and pilots, 2/Lieuts Taylor, Rose, Collier, Brandt, and Lieuts Leaver and Dickson.

Minchin's well-deserved DSO was gazetted on 1 January 1918. The squadron had maintained a high level of operational activity under his leadership and morale, by all accounts, had remained high under the most trying of circumstances and climatic conditions. There seems little doubt that Minchin's record as a field commander was outstanding and that this was clearly recognized by his superiors.

January also saw the arrival of SE5s and Sopwith Camels, which at long last would enable the squadron to compete on level terms with the 100mph Albatros and 120mph Halberstadt aircraft that had been flown by the enemy since September 1916. Indeed, given the squadron's record against these aircraft while flying technically inferior machines, there must have been some ingredient that enabled the pilots to maintain parity if not superiority.

The month saw the continuation of photo reconnaissance and bombing raids. A high spot was the attempt between 22 and 28 January to disable the German cruisers *Goeben* and *Breslau* which were attempting to escape into the Aegean. Operating with 17 Squadron

TRAVERS   BELL SCALES MINCHIN McBAIN RAMSON ROSS   BEENEY
D.F.C.   D.F.C. M.C.   D.S.O.M.C. M.C.   D.F.C.

'A' Flight 47 Squadron, March 1918

from Mudros, a claimed 15 tons of bombs were dropped in the face of strong defensive ack-ack fire. Unfortunately the bombs were too light, anti-personnel rather than armour-piercing, and the *Goeben* escaped. The *Breslau* struck mines and sank.

Once again the Macedonian winter rendered life difficult. In mid-February heavy snow falls collapsed a hangar at Hadzi-Junas aerodrome. Two BE12s and a Vickers Bullet were destroyed and two Vickers Bullets, an SE5a and a newly arrived Bristol M.1c were damaged.

Minchin's time with 47 Squadron was almost up. On 13 March, he relinquished his command to Major GD Gardner, MC, pausing only to have his photograph taken with seven pilots from 'A' Flight. Then he was homeward bound.

Perhaps H Collinson Owen, official correspondent in the Near East, in his book *Salonica and After* (1919) best summed up the role played by the Allied airmen in this campaign:

In common with the rest of the Salonica forces, very little had been heard of them at home. In activity and dash they were far and away ahead of anything else on the Balkan front . . . their superiority was so obvious to anybody who knew anything of the results obtained on the Balkan front that little was said about the Allied aviators at all. They had helped all they could in the battle, flying at heights of less than three hundred feet on contact patrols, in and out of clouds of dust and smoke, maintaining contact with the infantry while themselves being hundreds of feet below the enemy machine gunners on the Ridge and Grand Couronné . . . For over two years our aviators in the Balkans worked under a very great handicap. They had to be content with what machines were left over at home, and on these had to face enemy aviators flying greatly superior machines. It was only that wonderful and mysterious 'something' which marks the British aviator out from all others which enabled them to more than hold their own.

Chapter Nine

Wing Commander

By 5 April 1918 Minchin was back in England, with the acting rank of Lt Col.[27] He was based near Maidstone in Kent, in command, according to his service record, of 6 Wing, RAF, a part of No 1 Group, RAF. The Wing had been formed at Dover in August 1915 but moved around a lot in the next few years. No 1 Group was officially formed in June 1918 as a Training Group with HQ in London and, in early July 1918, 6 Wing was re-organised and based at Dover, Wye and Manston and these were

A Bristol M.1c

---

[27] Traditionalists from the RFC were notoriously slow to adopt the new RAF rank designations and Minchin never did. Lieutenant Colonel equated to a Wing Commander in the new RAF.

probably its station bases, though it had been occupying locations in Kent for some time previously. It would seem that between April and July it was in a state of re-organisation, though probably continuing its training role.

According to Harry:

He had several cars at his disposal and a beautiful WRAF chauffeuse. In July he became engaged to a girl from Maidstone [*Flight* announced his engagement to Margarita Beatrice White of Maidstone in 1918] *but this did not last long and was soon broken off. She was pretty and well off but not quite a lady. Jack about this time was drawing a very good salary and being so near London he indulged his propensity for that riotous company that always welcomed him but which had not a good effect on him. He got engaged several times but all these engagements led to nothing.*

The armistice was signed on the 11 November and on 19 November Minchin was posted to command 89 Wing in France, consisting of 32, 45 and 94 Squadrons, which had been operating in the area of the Somme in France. One of his squadron commanders was Major Trafford Leigh-Mallory[29].

Three weeks later, on 19 December, he sent a strongly worded report to Headquarters, 3rd Brigade, RAF, complaining bitterly about the personnel that he found staffing Wing HQ. In it he enumerated the 34 other ranks who staffed the Wing and spelled out each one's unsuitability for his post. For example, of his three motorcyclists, he says:

These men are utterly inefficient and have no knowledge of motor cycles beyond what was given at a two week course. No military training and never been overseas before. A break-down occurs every time a long journey is made, and despatches are often in consequence delayed two days. One man is at present awaiting trial by Court Martial for negligently losing his motor cycle and side car.

He received a fairly dusty reply from Brigade which pointed out that the war was over and that the personnel were awaiting demobilisation.

---

[29] Later Air Chief Marshal Sir Trafford Leigh-Mallory, KCB, DSO, who would command 12 Group, Fighter Command, in the Battle of Britain and become Air C in C for the invasion of Normandy. He was brother to George Mallory, the mountaineer, who died on Everest.

His remaining duties, late in December 1918, were to identify recommendations for promotion and then in January to make recommendations for the Peace Honours List. With less than two months in post, his views on these matters must have depended heavily on advice from his staff. Demobilisation was beginning and the administration of this also fell to his lot.

Chapter Ten

52 Wing

On 10 February 1919 Minchin was transferred to Home Establishment pending his next posting. This followed within days, as on 16 February he joined an Expeditionary Force destined for India. He was to command 52 Wing, engaged on internal security patrols along the Afghan border and Waziristan. This was another geographically demanding posting. Waziristan is a mountainous province on the North West Frontier of India, some 160 by 60 miles in size. Its western border flanks Afghanistan along the Suleiman mountains, while its eastern runs down the Indus plain to the river Indus. It is populated by four main tribes, all Pathans: the Wazirs, Mahsuds, Daurs and Bhittanis, all of whom had been implacable warrior foes of the British Raj for well over 100 years. Climatically, it is extreme, with temperatures ranging from 120°F in the plains to near freezing in the hills or at altitude. Cholera, dysentry and lesser stomach bugs were prevalent while the sun, scorpions and sandflies rendered life uncomfortable, if not dangerous.

While Minchin was en route, on 20 February Afghanistan's pro-British ruler, Amir Habibullah Khan, was assassinated. His son Amir Amanullah Khan seized power, sweeping aside Habibullah's younger brother Nasrullah, the lawful heir, and sought to incite nationalistic expectations, with the aim of achieving independence from India and from Britain.

Arriving at Bombay on 14 March 1919, by 30 March Minchin had reached Lahore – to find a highly unstable political situation. The Indian government refused to recognise Afghanistan's independence and, on 3 May 1919, hostilities had broken out along the border. Minchin's 52 Wing, due to consist of two squadrons and part of a third, had yet to arrive from the UK. By 2 April he was at Quetta 'on inspection duty'. Eventually, equipped with some tired aircraft from the Western Front, still bearing their patched bullet holes, 20 Squadron with 18 Bristol F2bs arrived at Bombay on 6 June and by 16 June had assembled at Risalpur.

A Handley Page V/1500, sister to *Old Carthusian*

Soon dispersed to Parachinar and Bannu, as well as Risalpur, with one flight at Tank, 20 Squadron was ready. 99 Squadron with nine DH9As and three DH10s, had arrived at Ambala, in the eastern Punjab, on 15 June. On 8 July Minchin moved from RAF HQ Simla to HQ Peshawar 'on completion of temporary duty'.

On 21 July 20 Squadron moved to Parachinar, west of Peshawar, on the Afghan border close to the Khyber Pass, only to move again on 22 September to Bannu, north eastern Waziristan, north of Dera Ismael Khan, where 52 Wing HQ was based. On 30 September 99 Squadron moved from Ambala, where it had been since mid-June, to Mianwali in the western Punjab, across the Indus from Dera Ismael Khan.

One flight from 97 Squadron equipped with DH10s did not arrive at Allahabad until 13 August. This was an inauspicious start to Minchin's command and his frustration must have been extreme. Already based in India, but not a part of 52 Wing, were 31 Squadron at Risalpur and 114 Squadron at Lahore.

The May hostilities along the Afghan border lasted just four weeks. During that time Afghan troops, assisted by thousands of tribesmen, engaged troops of the British and Indian armies. RAF aircraft were used for reconnaissance, artillery spotting and low level strafing in support of the troops. This activity had its dangers, for the Pathan tribesman were fine marksmen. Hostilities were effectively brought to a close by a vast prototype Handley Page long range bomber, the V/1500, J1936, nicknamed *Old Carthusian*. The name was chosen by one of the two pilots who had flown the aircraft from England to India via France, Italy, Malta, Egypt, Baghdad, Karachi and Delhi to Lahore. This was Major ASC MacLaren[29], educated at Charterhouse School (hence the name), who piloted the aircraft together with an ex-RNAS veteran, Capt Robert 'Jock' Halley. On 13 May the aircraft was flown on from Lahore to Risalpur where it was fitted with bomb racks, removed from 31 Squadron BEs. On 24 May, *Old Carthusian* took off for its first and last sortie, piloted by Halley with Lt FEE Villiers (later Sir Edward Villiers) as his bomb aimer, laden with possibly 7500lbs of 112 and 20 lb bombs. Flying along the Khyber Pass, it reached Kabul, the Afghan capital, and scored several direct hits including three on Amanullah's palace and one on his harem. *Old Carthusian's* fraught six hour journey to Kabul and back (there had been engine problems) brought Amanullah to the conference table on 3 June, followed by an armistice. A peace treaty was signed on 8 August 1919. *Old Carthusian* never flew again due to the depredations of termites which weakened its wing spars, but it lived on as a squadron office at Risalpur for some years. Halley records that he was directly responsible to the AOC India but, as he would receive an extra 100 rupees a month if he served west of the Indus, he wangled a temporary transfer to 31 Squadron. The giant V/1500 might have served well had the war in Europe lasted a few more months. As it was, this was the only offensive action ever flown by the type, which was withdrawn from service in January 1920.

The Official Account of the Third Afghan War stated that:

The machines [from 31 and 114 Squadrons], *with which the RAF were equipped when the Third Afghan War broke out, were obsolete and worn out. Their climbing power was low, and this led to their being shot at from the hill-tops as they passed along the valleys.*
[On 14 January 1920 20 Squadron was to lose three F2bs to rifle fire, four of the six crew members losing their lives]. *Their moral effect, however, was undoubtedly great, and the bombing of Dakka, Jalalabad and especially Kabul were factors which probably decided the Amir to sue for peace. The greatest credit is due to the officers of the Royal Air Force for the courage and skill which they displayed in performing their duties in these antiquated machines.*

---

[29] MacLaren had served with Minchin in 14 Squadron (see pages 44 and 46).

Peace treaties meant little. By December 1919 Afghan tribesmen were again active. De Watteville, in his book *The Waziristan Campaign of 1919-20*, states that on 20 December, after a reverse in the fighting against the hostile Mahsuds in the Tank Zam Valley:

> The entire resources of the RAF were called into play; four machines from 20 Squadron, six from 99 and three from 97 were allocated to bombing and machine gun work in support of the troops, and carried out twenty-seven flights over Mandanna Hill during the whole operation, that is, until 1700 hrs. Six machines flew up the valley bombing all parties of the enemy in sight.

This operation was known as the Battle of Mandanna Hill, and is frequently cited as an early example of Army/RAF joint operations. De Watteville goes on to comment that 'the aeroplane in 1919-20 was found to be a valuable complement to the rifle, the gun and the howitzer' and praises the RAF liaison officer at Military HQ. Might this have been Minchin?

On 1 August 1919 Minchin was granted a permanent commission as a Squadron Leader, an extraordinarily generous recognition of his achievements as an operational commander. Several airmen who went on to achieve Air rank were not treated as generously. However, reluctant to face what he perceived as the tedium of peacetime service, he appears to have resigned his commission on 11 November 1919. From 10 February until 2 March 1920 he was granted 23 days' privilege leave and on 4 March 1920 he was transferred to the United Kingdom for demobilisation. He retired an acting Wing Commander, though he continued to use his equivalent RFC rank of Lieutenant Colonel.

Some authorities refer to a Wing Commander RP Mills, MC, AFC, as being the overall RAF group commander in India[30]. This suggests that Minchin, in command of 52 Wing, may have been subordinate to him.

Minchin's service record reports him as commanding 52 Wing until 8 July 1919 when he is transferred to RAF HQ. Then on 24 July he apparently moved from Simla to Peshawar on 'Temporary Duty'. On

---

[30] On 20 September 1919 the rank of RAF commander in India was raised to Air Commodore, the first such air officer being Air Commodore (later Air Vice Marshal Sir) TI Webb-Bowen, CB, CMG.

14 November (5 November according to Squadron records) he moved from HQ 52 Wing to HQ India, then back to 52 Wing at Dera Ismail Khan; thence in swift succession to Risalpur, Lahore and Manzai. He relinquished command of 52 Wing on 20 January 1920.

On 15 March 1920 the supplement to the London Gazette carried the following report:

> *The 31st Squadron, Royal Air Force, under the direction of Lieutenant-Colonel F.F.Minchin, D.S.O., M.C., Commanding the 52nd Wing, carried out concentrated bombing raids on Jalalabad on the 17th, 20th and 24th May with marked effect; large portions of the military quarter of the town were burnt out, including the Afghan headquarters, and on one occasion a parade of 2000 Afghan troops was bombed with good results. In the panic which followed these raids the neighbouring tribesmen entered the town and secured large quantities of loot in the shape of arms, ammunition and treasure. On the 24th, Captain Halley, R.A.F., in a Handley-Page machine, performed a notable feat by bombing Kabul; and there is little doubt that this raid was an important factor in producing a desire for peace at the headquarters of the Afghan Government.*

Minchin sailed for England during the month of March.

Chapter Eleven

Civilian Life

According to Harry Minchin, on board ship on the way home Jack lost at cards much of the money that he had saved in India. The rest soon went on his arrival in London in April 1920 when he chose to stay at the Cavendish Hotel in Jermyn Street, a place notorious for its high cost of living and for the raffish type of person who frequented it.

We have to assume that Minchin whiled away most of the next five months living in London and socialising in a fashion that would quickly erode his modest finances. Although Harry has proved to be a less-than-wholly reliable biographer, we have largely to rely on his account of this period in Minchin's life. He records that his brother became friendly with a man called Selby-Lowndes who:

Helped him spend his money and took him round all the gay spots in London. They stayed with Selby-Lowndes' parents [Mr and Mrs Meyrick Selby-Lowndes of Mursley Grange, Winslow, Bucks] *and during one of these visits Jack met Betty Selby-Lowndes, their daughter, and became smitten. She was a most beautiful girl and a born lady, but also a conspicuous member of a notorious and very fast set. She for her part was very attracted to this tall, very good looking, distinguished, and most simple young man. Jack bought a Vauxhall car and he took her about in this to various country houses and they got engaged.*

The engagement was announced, belatedly, in *The Eastbournian*, the Eastbourne College magazine, in July 1921.

During the summer of 1920 Minchin and Betty visited Annagh with 'Swilby', as young Selby-Lowndes was known. Harry's narrative continues:

After some weeks Betty went back to England. Then 'Swilby' decided to go too and asked Jack to lend him the money for his fare. Jack

In 1920

would not do this but offered him his car, to drive from Holyhead, where it was garaged, to London. 'Swilby' agreed to do this, took the car to London and sold it there as his own, and Jack never saw it again. Jack was in a great fix over this but he did not want to expose Betty's brother, but he wanted the car or the money. He approached the Selby-Lowndes relations but could get nothing done.

During the visit to Annagh with Betty, Lena, his stepmother, was very offensive to Minchin, so much so that he packed his bags and left Annagh for Murraghboro' House, Puckane, where his Aunt Georgie Bruce, his father's sister, looked after him for four weeks. He refused to set foot in Annagh while his stepmother was there.

Harry points out that his brother had survived a violent and dangerous war and was very nervy from 'war strain'. As the younger son, he had no inheritance to look forward to. He had lost his mother when only 14, while his much-loved grandfather had died in 1916. His father, to whom he had never been close, had married again and his family home, Annagh, was no longer his home. He was, by his own decision, no longer *persona grata* there. And his finances were at a low ebb. The outlook was bleak.

Perhaps his gloom was slightly relieved when on 12 July 1920 his CBE was gazetted 'for services in India'. This was certainly awarded in recognition of the part that he had played while commanding 52 Wing in the operations on the North West Frontier in 1919 and was a remarkable

Betty

accolade for such a young and comparatively junior officer. *The London Gazette* showed his rank as Squadron Leader (A/Wing Cmdr) although he had already resigned his commission..

On 1 October 1920 Minchin and Betty were married at the Register Office in the District of St Martin[31], in London. He was 30, and gave his address as the Cavendish Hotel, Jermyn Street. Betty, just 20, gave her address as Mursley Grange, Winslow. The marriage certificate makes it clear that Betty was young Selby-Lowndes' sister and not his cousin, as Harry had it. The witnesses to the ceremony were named Thompson and Tomkins and were probably either employees at the Register Office or casual passers-by. Consequently it is reasonable to assume that the wedding was attended by no member of either family although, as a minor, Betty would have needed her parents' permission to marry. Harry later recorded that the marriage had taken place in Dublin, so clearly he was not present.

When the war ended the RAF shrank almost immediately. 188 squadrons and 22,647 aircraft were reduced to a mere 33 squadrons. About 291,000 airmen of all ranks (plus approximately 25,000 WRAF) were demobilized and in search of employment.

Harry states that it was through Betty's influence that Minchin was introduced to Sir Edward Sassoon, who offered him a job working in

---

[31] This was located at the south end of St Martin's Lane, WC2.

his offices in Calcutta. Sir Edward was chief partner in E Sassoon & Co., merchants and bankers of India, London and China and was already 67 years of age. It has to be wondered whether a girl of 20 was likely to be on intimate terms with a businessman of his age and substance. His son Victor had served in the RNAS, reaching the rank of Flight Commander, so it may be that the introduction to Minchin came about from that direction, rather than through Betty. Whichever was the case, in the same month in which he was married (October), Minchin set sail for India. His impulsive and ill-assorted marriage was already floundering. Indeed Betty would later claim that they had never lived together. Minchin was in no position to support her in the style to which she aspired. In consequence, she did not accompany him to India and was soon known to be living under the protection of a wealthy man, Major Jack Fielden, whom some years later she married.

En route to Calcutta, Minchin's ship docked at Colombo where Harry's ship was in port and this provided an opportunity for a brotherly reunion.

Chapter Twelve

A Civilian in India

Arriving in Calcutta early in 1921, Minchin at first shared a house with Lt Col Ivo Arthyr Edwards. Edwards, a professional soldier and artillery officer some nine years older than Minchin, had transferred to the Royal Flying Corps in 1916 and risen to the rank of Wing Commander (as had Minchin) before leaving the RAF in 1919.

Minchin seems initially to have worked hard and attempted to learn Hindustani. No doubt he 'played hard' too, for that was his style. He is recorded as playing a lot of tennis and among his friends, for example, were the lovely daughters of the Maharajah of Cooch Behar. Somehow he acquired an Avro 504K which he kept at Dum Dum airport, and in this he recorded 83 hours' flying time. However, according to brother Harry: 'Jack's troubles started afresh, for he had by now acquired expensive tastes and all his savings were spent, War Gratuity gone, and the £1000 odd that his grandfather had left him was too tied up for him to be able to use.'

Thereafter we are dependent on the recollections of former Fairey test pilot and aviation author Captain Norman Macmillan, MC, AFC[32]. On 24 May 1922 Macmillan had set off from Croydon in a DH9 (G-EBDE) in an attempted round-the-world flight using a separate aircraft for each of four stages. He was accompanied by Major Wilfred T Blake, the expedition leader, and a Lt Col LE Broome as cine-photographer. Blake, who had landed at Agra with suspected appendicitis, travelled on to Calcutta by train and, arriving ahead of Macmillan, met Minchin at Dum Dum. Consequently he and Blake were there to meet the DH9 when it landed on Saturday 12 August. Earlier Minchin had taken Blake up in his Avro and flown in the direction of Gaya to try to meet Macmillan, only to be forced by the weather conditions to return to Dum Dum.

---

[32] A full account of the episode that follows is to be found in *Freelance Pilot*, by Norman Macmillan (Heinemann, 1937).

At Calcutta the DH9 was disposed of and a Fairey IIIC seaplane (G-EBDI), which had been prepared by the RAF for the next stage of the journey to Vancouver, was made ready. Meanwhile Blake entered Calcutta General Hospital to have his appendix removed and Broome went on to Japan by ship to prepare for their arrival there. Photographer Geoffrey H Malins[33] was recruited to take Broome's place.

Taking off on 19 August from the Hugli river at Calcutta in the Fairey, Macmillan soon met with headwinds which reduced his groundspeed to less than 50mph. Abandoning his original 350 mile course for Akyab on the other side of the Bay of Bengal, he set a new course for Chittagong. Worse was to befall. Engine failure forced a landing onto seas which were running eight foot waves. Despite managing to restart the engine, take-off was impossible and the aircraft was taxied in the direction of the mudflat island of Lukhidia Char. There they were to remain for two days and three nights, precariously balanced on the sodden Fairey, burnt raw by the sun by day, wet and cold by night. Macmillan eventually managed to persuade an English-speaking native who had approached in his sampan to carry a telegram to the nearest post office, some 25 miles away. The message read as follows:

DOWN ONE MILE SOUTH OF LUKHIDIA CHAR. LAT. 22-15¾ N., LONG. 91-12 E. ENGINE FAILURE. ALL O.K. NOW. PETROL SHORT OWING TO HEAVY ADVERSE WIND. ADVISE CHITTAGONG TO KEEP LOOK OUT FOR US FROM HIGH TIDE TUESDAY AND OBTAIN PETROL. ADVISE ALL CONCERNED. LIVING ON MILK SUPPLIED BY NATIVES IN EXCHANGE FOR CIGARS.

CHEERIO. MAC AND MALINS.

Because of Blake's recent operation, he addressed it to Minchin in Calcutta.

After managing briefly on the Tuesday to become airborne again, they soon had to ditch and their aircraft drifted slowly towards land, eventually turning turtle, and it was only the arrival on 24 August of the harbour-master, one Cummings, from Chittagong in a British-manned

---

[33] Malins was a famous photographer who had been responsible for the cine-film of the mine exploding under the Hawthorne Redoubt in the Battle of the Somme on 1 July 1916.

steam launch that saved the two men's lives. Minchin, on receiving the telegram, had taken it to Blake in Calcutta General Hospital and he sent it on to the news editor of the *Calcutta Statesman* which had local rights to the expedition's story. The editor then sent a less than urgent version of the message to Chittagong. It was this rather nonchalant message that stimulated the rescue mission. It has to be admitted that Macmillan's telegram, in view of their plight, was scarcely pressing and this in essence was the message that was relayed to Chittagong. Much later, in *Wings of Fate (1967)*, a book dedicated to Minchin among others, Macmillan wrote:

> *Minchin afterwards told me that he regretted not sending the complete message to Chittagong himself as soon as he received my cable, but he had felt the correct thing to do was to take the cable to Blake straight away since he was leader of the expedition. I believe Minchin inwardly chided himself for having been partly instrumental in putting our lives in jeopardy by following channels of communication instead of taking direct action.*

The remainder of the plans for the round-the-world flight were abandoned.

Minchin's father had died on 15 August 1922 and he immediately got in touch with Gunner and Gillson, the family solicitors, to try to get his hands on the £1000[34] that his grandfather had left him. Unfortunately this was prevented by Major Harry Lefroy, his uncle. At about this time, Harry Minchin's ship put into Colombo and Minchin travelled to join him on board for a fortnight. Harry wrote: 'Jack was looking ill and worried and he was in debt.' Betty was starting divorce proceedings and, as Harry recorded: 'Jack decided to return to England and if necessary chuck up Sassoons. He did both.'

---

[34] This sum was worth some £35,000 in today's money.

Chapter Thirteen

Back in England

Minchin sailed for England early the following year, 1923. Once there, he lodged at first with Ivo Edwards, with whom he had shared a house in Calcutta. Edwards had become Chief Technical Adviser at the Air Ministry and wrote later that Minchin 'stayed with me [at Sevenoaks] for a considerable time while he was looking for a job'.

It seems that Minchin travelled to Annagh at this time because Harry records that he 'arrived back in Ireland during the bad times.' The 'bad times' refers to the Civil War which from April 1922 until April 1923 was waged between the rebels or Irregulars and the Provisional Government. Thurles, about twelve miles from Annagh, had seen bitter fighting in July 1922 and in January 1923 the Republicans attacked and sometimes burned the country houses (such as Annagh) of supposed supporters of the Irish Free State.

Annagh had been raided the night before Minchin's arrival and as he drove up in a motor car, rather late at night, without having warned them, he was refused admittance. It may be that the household was simply being cautious rather than knowingly denying him entrance. So he drove on to Murraghboro' where they were delighted to see him.

However the family welcome was muted. As Harry wrote:

Family conferences galore then sat on Jack's affairs, all of which were profuse with abuse but barren of all really practical suggestions of help.

Jack's situation now rapidly progressed from bad to worse. In a despairing attempt to settle his debts Minchin had borrowed money from a former Irish Guards officer.

Jack borrowed money from this man on the strength of the money left him by our grandfather that was still in trust. What the exact terms were I do not know, but for about £120 Jack made over his reversionary interest in this £1000 to this man. Jack did this without in the least realizing what he was doing. Jack charged this unscrupulous Guardsman with having obtained money by false pretences, but the case was never brought up, Jack having really no leg to stand on, for he had been defrauded entirely through his own stupidity.

Minchin at this time undertook to provide Betty with evidence whereby the divorce that she wanted could be concluded. The 1925 divorce petition revealed that on 21/22 February 1923 he, while resident at the Norris Mansion hotel in the Haymarket, London, committed adultery with an unknown woman. This, as Harry later insisted, was a quixotic and probably synthetic gesture by Minchin, but not uncommon given the divorce laws of the time.

Minchin must also have made contact with Norman Macmillan who later wrote 'Minchin came to England the following year. I introduced him to many of my friends and he was happy with them and they with him. He was seeking a post in British aviation and I introduced him to the Bristol Aviation Company. But he had no experience of test flying and later joined Imperial Airways as a transport pilot.' Clearly Minchin was seeking a post in the emergent business of civil aviation. First he had to obtain a Commercial Pilot's Licence. On 8 January he passed his commercial licence medical, was pronounced 'Fit for Reserve' and was shortly after gazetted a Flying Officer in the RAF Reserve of Officers. He was granted Civil Licence No.371 on 13 February 1924 and this

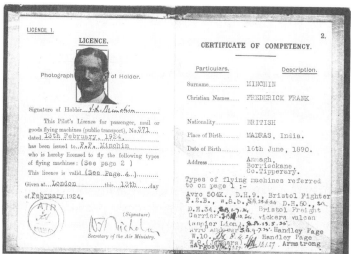

Minchin's civil licence

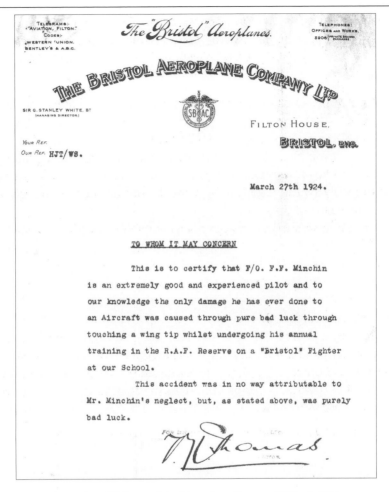

Letter from HJ Thomas, Bristol Aeroplane Company 27 March 1924

authorized him to fly the Avro 504K, the DH9 and the Bristol Fighter F2B. From 13 until 22 February 1924 Minchin underwent his first annual training at the Bristol RAFO Flying School. His assessment[35] read: 'Good average pilot. Landed cross-wind after cross-country flight and wrecked machine [Bristol Fighter F2B]. Passed as category 2.' Later a Mr HJ Thomas of the Bristol Aeroplane Company wrote of the incident as being 'pure bad luck through touching a wing tip . . . in no way attributable to Mr Minchin's neglect.'

---

[35] To be found under Air 76/350 at the National Archives.

26/3/24.

To whom it may concern.

Lt. Colonel F.F. Minchin served under my command as a flight commander in Egypt during 1916. I found him an excellent pilot, & an intelligent and zealous officer. I have no hesitation in recommending him for a position either as pilot or for ground duties in an air transport concern.

P.B. Joubert
Group Captain.
Royal Air Force.

Minchin's letter of recommendation from Philip Joubert

Jack was desperate to find employment, preferably in aviation, and must have canvassed some of his RFC and RAF superiors. Philip Joubert responded positively with the commendatory letter illustrated here.

However storm clouds had already begun to gather. On 2 January 1924 his creditors filed for him to be declared bankrupt and on the 12th the Receiving Order for his bankruptcy appeared in the *London Gazette*. His address was listed as '11 Grosvenor Gardens, Mews East, Victoria, lately residing at the Birch Hotel, Haywards Heath'. The Date of Bankruptcy Order was recorded as 31 March 1924, with 7 May set as the Date of Public Examination. Alfred Everard, accountant, of 151 North Street, Brighton, was appointed by the court as trustee to the case.

In April, Harry returned to England to find his brother 'starving and living in squalor near Euston Station[36]. He was in debt to his landlady and had sold or pawned all his spare clothes.'

---

[36] Harry may have meant Victoria Station.

Chapter Fourteen

Civil Aviation

In 1919 and the early 1920s the emergence of civil aviation as a commercial reality was due to the entrepreneurial courage of small companies operating aircraft such as the DH4, the DH9 and the Vickers Vimy which had been designed for and possibly used for military purposes and which had been hurriedly adapted to carry passengers. These first companies were Air Transport and Travel (AT&T), founded in 1916 but which ceased operations on 17 December 1920; a subsidiary of S Instone & Co, ship-owners, (later to become Instone Air Line); Handley Page Transport; Daimler Airway (founded in 1922) and the British Marine Air Navigation Company, which operated amphibious Supermarines out of Southampton. At first the land-based airlines flew from Hounslow, Hendon and Cricklewood until Croydon was adopted as the Customs Airport of London on 29 March 1920. It had been used since 1915 by the Royal Flying Corps as a part of the air defence of London and later by the RAF for pilot training.

Parallel with these developments, there existed opinion which believed that the future of air travel lay with the airship, widely used for observation and bombing in the recent war. Quiet, smooth, reliable and with luxurious accommodation, they were everything that the noisy and accident-prone aircraft were not. Two of the first were the British R33 and R34, launched in 1919, in which year the latter had flown to America and back. The American USS *Shenandoah* flew in 1923 and was the first to be inflated with helium. The USS *Los Angeles* flew for eight years. The German *Graf Zeppelin* left on a round-the-world trip on 1 August 1929 during which it covered 21,000 miles. Between 1928 and 1935 the *Graf* made 505 trips and covered over a million miles. The privately funded R100, designed by Barnes Wallis with assistant Neville Shute Norway (later to find fame as a novelist), went on its maiden flight to Canada and back in 1930. It was the disastrous crash of the publicly funded but inadequately tested R101 near Beauvais on 6 October 1930, which killed Lord Thomson and Sir Sefton Brancker, and the German *Hindenburg* disaster at Lakehurst on 6 May 1937 which finally put paid to the airship saga.

However it soon became apparent that government-subsidized foreign competition was rendering the Croydon operation uneconomic and by February 1921 all flying by British airlines ceased. By March a scheme of government subsidy had been worked out and Handley Page and Instone recommenced flying on routes which avoided uneconomic overlapping. By October 1922 Daimler was running a Manchester–Croydon–Amsterdam service. The aircraft flown were DH34 10-seaters, DH18 8-seaters, a Vickers Vulcan 8-seater, converted Handley Page 0/400 bombers and a Handley Page W8b.

A Handley Page W8b

In 1923 the Government's concern over subsidies led to the establishment of the Hambling Committee to consider the future of air transport. It recommended that there should be a single British commercial company which would incorporate all the companies then existing. And so on 1 April 1924 Imperial Airways was born. The initial team of pilots was Bill

Armstrong, FJ Bailey, Franklyn Barnard (later appointed Chief Pilot), Freddie Dismore, CF Wolley Dodd, Ray Hinchliffe[37], Herbert Horsey, OP Jones, Robert H McIntosh, Minchin, Gordon Olley[38] George Powell, AL 'Scruffy' Robinson, HS Robertson, Walter Rogers, LA Wates, Arthur Wilcockson and 'Jimmy' Youell, many of whom were to become household names in the years to come. All were former RFC or RNAS pilots and all, with the exception

1924

of Minchin[39], had already established track records as civil pilots with the predecessor firms.

Although it has been written that Minchin first flew for the Instone Air Line, given that he did not gain his civil licence until 13 February 1924, it seems almost certain that he joined Imperial Airways[40]on its formation[41] – when it absorbed Instone. Indeed, it was not until 1 July 1924 that he added the DH34 to his commercial licence. The first type conversion on Minchin's commercial licence was for a Handley Page W8b on 23 May 1924 which makes it virtually impossible that he was absorbed into Imperial from the existing airlines. However join he did, at or very near the setting up of Imperial Airways. It seems that he was almost immediately greeted with a pilots' strike when Imperial's offer of a small basic salary of £100 pa plus 2d per mile flown was rejected

---

[37] Hinchliffe had served with 10 (later 210) Squadron RNAS and, flying Camels, had achieved six victories, which qualified him as an 'ace'. He was awarded the DFC before a serious crash caused the loss of his left eye. He thereafter he wore an eye patch.

[38] Joining the RFC as a dispatch rider, Olley served as a Sergeant pilot in 1 Squadron, recording ten victories between June and October 1917, making him an 'ace'. He was awarded the MM.

[39] There were inaccurately captioned postcard photographs which suggest that Minchin flew for Instone.

[40] His appointment was supported in letters written on 26 March 1924 by Air Marshals Sir Sefton Brancker and Geoffrey Salmond, and by Philip Joubert.

[41] Harald Penrose, in *Wings across the World* (Cassell 1980), refers (inaccurately) to Minchin 'returning to the fold'.

The Croydon caricatures

During the 1920s, artist, illustrator and aviation enthusiast Charles Couper Dickson was closely connected with Croydon Airport and produced a large number of caricatures of the personalities of all kind who worked at the aerodrome. These at one time hung in the Pilots' Room at the Aerodrome Hotel and some are still displayed in the hotel to this day. Sadly Minchin's is not among them. Dickson wrote in his 1985 biography 'My most exhilarating flights ...were in DH34s with Minchin and pink eye-shaded Hinchliffe'.

by the pilots who had been accustomed to receive between £800 and £1000 pa from their former employers. A delegation was sent to the new Secretary of State for Air, Lord Thomson. One source[42] asserts that in 1924 Minchin was President of the newly-formed Pilots' Federation with Franklyn Barnard as Secretary. This is not wholly impossible, as Minchin, with his military rank and decorations, might well have been seen as a suitably grand figurehead for the new trades union. Eventually, and after the involvement of the TUC, salaries were set at a maximum of £880 per annum with life assurance of £1000. In consequence of these delays, Imperial did not actually begin flying until 28 April.

While the four week strike was in process, Minchin improved his finances by sky-writing advertisements over London. When flying resumed and because of the new pay scheme, he began, in an effort to improve his precarious finances, accumulating more flying hours than any other pilot. He also took up residence in the Trust House hotel at Croydon, next door to the aerodrome. This provided, as Robert McIntosh (popularly known as 'All-Weather Mac' due to his apparent ability to navigate his HP 0/400 in impenetrable fog) later recorded in his memoirs:[43]

---

[42] *Airship Navigator* by EA Johnston (Skyline 1994)
[43] *All-Weather Mac* by RH McIntosh, DFC, AFC (Macdonald & Co 1963).

A cheerful service-like atmosphere. When we were on duty, life was tough enough and we took on responsibilities of no mean weight. But off duty we relaxed and had a lot of fun. Most of the unmarried pilots lived in the makeshift Trust House hotel on the aerodrome itself ... We often took our drinks into the only warm room in the hotel, which was the kitchen. Freddie Minchin, when the chef's eye was diverted one evening, removed the lid from the stockpot simmering on the range boiling up bones for the morrow's soup. He sniffed the contents and thought they could do with some improvement. He tipped his drink into the pot. This seemed a good idea and everyone else did the same, whisky, port, brandy, sherry, the lot, it all went in. The hotel served a 1/6d [7½p] lunch for aerodrome staff and, on the next day: *The management were amazed to see the restaurant filled with pilots, engineers, control and office staff, all in various stages of hilarity or undue post-prandial somnolence.*

Minchin, as was not-uncommon with former Royal Flying Corps pilots, had, as the aviation writer Major MS Marsden put it in a *Sunday Graphic* article, 'two characters – on parade and off parade. When he was working, his whole mind was on the job; when he had time to kill, he would set out to get the greatest amusement out of his leisure.' It was the Old Oundelian Cecil Lewis MC who said in *Sagittarius Rising*[44], his classic account of World War One flying, that 'The RFC attracted the adventurous spirits, the devil-may-care young bloods of England, the fast livers, the furious drivers – men who were not happy unless they were taking risks.'

McIntosh again:

Minchin was always in trouble of some sort or other, and often it was connected with his little German car. When it wouldn't start on the handle it was his practice to give it a shove and then take a flying leap into the driver's seat to engage the gear to start the engine. He did this one night at the top of Crown Hill in Croydon. On this occasion he should have first satisfied himself that the door would open.

---

[44] *Sagittarius Rising* by Cecil Lewis (Peter Davies 1936).

At Croydon

A more serious escapade led to Minchin appearing before Croydon magistrates charged with being drunk in charge of a motor car. Inspector Burke declared that he saw the Colonel, a few minutes after midnight, standing in front of the car and doing something to the engine. When spoken to, he (the Colonel) staggered to the front of the car and started laughing. At the Police Station, he had said 'If you say I'm bottled, I agree. I am pushing my car because I can't drive it.' The Inspector concluded his evidence by stating that the Colonel's behaviour throughout was exemplary and that of a gentleman. Speaking in his defence, Minchin said that when he left the Greyhound Hotel with a friend, the car would not start, so they decided to push it . . . and that, as he was not driving, there was no public danger. The magistrate must have agreed, and discharged him on payment of £1.15.0d (£1.75) costs.

These first commercial pilots needed to be robust. They frequently flew in open cockpits, were responsible for their own navigation (which was often a matter of following roads or railway lines[45]), had few or unreliable weather forecasts and enjoyed limited air traffic control. Radio, if it was fitted, was primitive and unreliable and forced landings[46] in small fields due to engine failure or to the weather were all too frequent. Indeed pilots were issued with a float of £5 or 500 francs known as 'forced landing money'. For passengers, the cabin was extremely noisy and there was no cabin heating or insulation. Seating comprised wicker chairs and few aircraft possessed a lavatory. Passengers needed to be brave, even foolhardy. However in the four and a half years between August 1919 and March 1924, British airlines carried 34,605 passengers and only five lost their lives, plus six crew.

There is no doubt that through most of 1924 Minchin was flying for Imperial. On 19 July, he had a slight accident in a de Havilland-owned DH50 (G-EBFO) while landing at Le Bourget. Damage repairs came to £43.14s.8d (£43.73). Then on 18 September, in a DH34 (G-EBBT), he struck a corrugated iron latrine after a 650 metre run while taking off heavily-laden from Bickendorf Aerodrome, Cologne, and buckled the undercarriage.

---

[45] A major disaster had occurred on 7 April 1922 when a DH18 of Daimler Airway collided with a Farman F.60 Goliath near Grandvilliers in France and all seven occupants perished. The two pilots had been following the Beauvais-Abbeville road on reciprocal courses.

[46] Gordon Olley claimed to have made 17 forced landings during one Croydon to Le Bourget flight. On his final take-off he was grieved to find that the last of his passengers had deserted him.

Minchin decided to use up his petrol and landed at Lympne where the local fire engine and ambulance were mustered in readiness. He made an excellent landing, albeit without wheels, and in so doing the floor of the cabin was completely removed, leaving the eight passengers seated on the grass. Three passengers were slightly injured and were compensated with payments amounting to £10. The damage to the aircraft amounted to £1100 which was covered by insurance. McIntosh, in *All-Weather Mac*, asserts that Minchin was known thereafter as 'Dan'. There are other memoirs which support this claim. Equally, others refer to him as Jack, Freddie or Minch. His was clearly a personality which inspired nicknames.

Far more seriously, on Christmas Eve 1924 a DH34 (G-EBBX), bound for Paris, crashed and caught fire on take-off just west of the Brighton road near Purley Oaks station with seven passengers on board. According to Archie Jackson[47], Hinchliffe had flown the aircraft, which was suffering from oil pressure problems, into Croydon from Amsterdam and refused to fly it back to Paris. The replacement pilot, Captain David Stewart, aged 34, and all seven passengers were killed. Minchin gave evidence at the enquiry held at the Law Courts in London on 30 January 1925, stating that the runway was not long enough, that the take-off was uphill and that the problem could be solved by removing certain of the buildings. There was considerable press interest in the enquiry and Minchin's evidence, in particular, was important in stimulating a major redevelopment of the airfield, finally completed in 1927. A memorial to those who lost their lives was placed in Lower Kingsdown Avenue, Purley, and was for many years visited on Christmas Eve by a lady, suspected to be Captain Stewart's widow, who placed flowers there. In June 2006 members of the Croydon Airport Society attached a small commemorative plaque to the memorial pillar.

Early that year, on the night of 7/8 February, Minchin again went through the charade at the Norris hotel in a further attempt to provide Betty with the evidence that she needed for her divorce petition. This was filed by her solicitor on 12 February and claimed that they had never lived together, nor co-habited, and cited Minchin's adultery, as the court required. The decree nisi was granted on 29 May, becoming absolute on 7 December 1925. Harry was aghast:

---

[47] *Old Pilots, Bold Pilots* by Archie Jackson (Cirrus Associates 1998).

Jack would be made to look an awful blackguard and was it fair on the family name which had been handed down to us spotless. Wasn't our family as good if not better than hers? Jack's views were entirely altruistic and chivalrous. He preferred to be in the right and yet to appear in the wrong, in order to spare her. Ye Gods spare her ! ! A lot she spared him.

In the end, Harry helped financially to produce the evidence required by the Divorce Court. He went on to say that:

During this period she was appearing at several notorious night clubs in London with the Earl of Birkenhead[48] . The sad part of this revolting business was that Jack loved his wife still, and yet so many of his friends and relations believed the evidence produced by the solicitors in order to obtain the divorce.

Despite the arduous, indeed dangerous, conditions, there can be little doubt that routine cross-Channel flying could become monotonous. 'Bus driving', some pilots called it. Others vied with one another to record the fastest crossings from Croydon to Cologne and to Paris. In 1922 'Cy' Holmes, a schoolfellow of Minchin's at Eastbourne College, had flown from Cologne to London for Instone, covering the 350 miles in 2hrs 39mins, an average speed of 132mph, and in so doing beat his own previous record time of 2hrs 55mins. On 15 August 1924 one-eyed Ray Hinchliffe, flying DH34 G-EBBW, recorded in his log book 'Overtook Minchin by flying shorter course over islands.' His log book for 25 February 1925 disclosed another contest: 'G-EBFC, Croydon, Amsterdam. I managed to beat Minchin in DH50 by 7 minutes.' A later attempt on the Paris record, again involving Hinchliffe[49], would have serious repercussions for Minchin (see page 120). For the more venturesome, there were new long distance routes to be explored and the Atlantic and other long distance flights or crossings to be achieved. The Atlantic had first been crossed by air, albeit in stages, by a US Navy Curtiss NC–4 flying boat between 8 and 13 May 1919. The first non-stop flight was achieved by Britons John Alcock and

---

[48] FE Smith, Lord Chancellor 1919–22, Secretary of State for India 1924-28.

[49] There can be little doubt that Minchin, Hinchliffe and other pilots waged a friendly war over the speed with which the Channel could be crossed. Hinchliffe's log books record two other instances of rivalry: he 'beat Travers by 20 minutes' on 18 May 1926, and on 7 August 1926 in a 'race with Wilcockson . . .he just beat me by 5 minutes.'

Arthur Whitten Brown on 14–15 June 1919 when they flew a Vickers Vimy bomber from Newfoundland to Clifden in County Galway, gaining a knighthood each and winning Lord Northcliffe's £10,000 prize. Soon after, between 2 and 12 July, the airship R34 made the first double crossing of the Atlantic by air. Between 4 February and 20 March 1920 Pierre van Ryneveld (a colleague of Minchin's in 14 Squadron and a participant in the El Arish raid) had in February/March 1920, with Christopher Quintin Brand, been the first to fly from Britain to South Africa in stages, using two Vickers Vimys and a DH9. As recorded earlier, in December 1918 and January 1919 Capts Norman Macmillan and Halley had flown the great Handley Page *Old Carthusian*[50] from England to India.

So there were challenges ahead and Minchin, with his low threshold of boredom and his instinctive need for challenge, was sooner or later going to grasp them. However, before this could happen, Minchin had one more adventure with an Imperial DH34 (G-EBBY). Flying a charter operation with a planeload of journalists in connection with the 804 mile King's Cup Air Race of 3–4 July 1925, he was forced by a dense sea mist and minimal visibility to land in a field at Carville near Durham. No-one was injured and the cost of repair to the DH34 came to £200 plus a £12 2s 0d (£12.10) insurance claim from a farmer for damage to a fence and some hay. *The Aeroplane* reported:

> *. . .after getting through all the bad fog in the south and getting further than any of the competitors who started early in the race, Col. Minchin ran into a bad patch of sea fret near the coast and tried to make a landing in what looked like a reasonable field. In the mist it was impossible to see that the field had a pronounced downward slope in the direction of landing and so the 34 continued its course till it crashed into a wood. Fortunately nobody was hurt.*

Minchin later reported the incident to Harry '. . .the blooming machine landed on the down slope and would not stop; it ran on and on and into a wood.' Not long after, Imperial decided that the DH34 was unsuitable for their work due to its 'heavy loading and bad unstick'. Abortive though it was, this was an interesting race. Competitors included Bert

---

[50] *Old Carthusian*'s exploits in India, for which Minchin may well have been the officer commanding, are described on pages 66 and 67.

The crash at Carville

At Croydon 1927

Hinkler, Alan Cobham, Frank Courtney and Franklyn Barnard (the eventual winner) and an interesting new aircraft, the Bristol Type 84 Bloodhound G-EBGG, which Minchin would fly himself before very long. One of Minchin's passengers on this occasion was James 'Jimmy' Jeffs, one of the first air traffic controllers at Croydon, who had a garden of which he was justly proud. As Bob McIntosh later recounted, he, with Minchin, 'Jimmy' Youell and two engineers, had once worked from midnight until the early hours and dug up all the prize shallots in Jimmy Jeffs' garden and re-planted them upside down.

A few days later, on 9 July, Minchin added the Avro Andover 563 to his licence. Specially built to replace the DH10 on the RAF's Cairo to Baghdad service, it was in fact used by Imperial on cross-Channel work from April 1925 until January 1927, when it joined the RAF as an air ambulance.

In August the Air Ministry announced that arrangements for a civil air route between Egypt and India had progressed and that a provisional agreement between the Ministry and Imperial Airways for the operation of a weekly service in each direction between Kantara and Karachi had been concluded. In early September Air Vice Marshal Sir Sefton Brancker, Director of Civil Aviation, left London for Port Said by the *SS Ranpura*. On the same day Minchin and a Colonel Burchall of Imperial Airways flew from Croydon to Paris, whence they travelled by train and ship to meet Brancker at Port Said. Minchin however was an undischarged bankrupt and, before they could depart, Harry had to put up a bail bond for him in the sum of £300 for his reappearance in England by a certain date, having 'put him on his word of honour to be back.'

Brancker arrived at Port Said on 2 September and met Minchin and Burchall at Alexandria. Flying a borrowed RAF Vickers Vernon, Minchin flew the party to Heliopolis where Brancker had a meeting with King Faud. The party continued to Ramleh in Palestine for talks with the AOC and officials before going on to Amman where Brancker was to meet King Abdullah. September 7 saw them fly on to Bagdhad for more meetings with British and Iraqi officials. On 10 September they flew on to Basra, then to Ahwaz and finally to Bushire. On 12 September Brancker returned to Bagdhad and finally Teheran while Minchin and Burchall continued to Karachi. By 1 October the survey was complete and Minchin and Burchall returned to Egypt to join Brancker on the

SS Helovan, bound for England. Brancker's report on the survey was generally optimistic though he rather underestimated the climatic, refuelling and maintenance difficulties that lay ahead, plus the need to establish landing grounds and emergency fuel depots where none existed. He was dubious about the use of the Vernon (a derivative of the Vimy Commercial), with its small payload and underpowered engines and, in due course, Imperial ordered four DH66 Hercules airliners, at a cost of £25,000 each, which began work on the Baghdad route on 18 December 1926. Proving flights were flown by three Imperial Captains: CF Wolley Dodd, Ray Hinchliffe and Franklyn Barnard, and the service began in earnest on 12 January 1927.

While Minchin was away with Brancker, Napier, the aero engine manufacturers, ran a full page advertisement (illustrated) in *The Aeroplane* of 16 September in which Minchin extolled the virtues of their engines. He was quoted as saying:

100,000 miles on Napier engines ! by one Pilot ♦

Col. F. F. Minchin, D.S.O., the experienced pilot of Imperial Airways has covered over 100,000 miles (1000 hours) on Napier water cooled engines on commercial service.

The following is an extract from a recent letter to us :—

"Throughout the whole of this period I have never had a forced landing from engine failure, or experienced any engine trouble whatever.

It is my opinion that the Napier is unquestionably the best aero engine of to-day. During the whole of my flying experience of thirteen years, I have never before experienced such consistent reliability."

Napier Engines Ensure Reliability.

NAPIER
Water Cooled Aero Engines

D. NAPIER & SON, LTD.
Acton Vale, London, W.3

An advertisement for Napier aero engines

On 16 September 1925 *The Aeroplane* magazine ran an advertisement by Napier which employed Minchin's growing fame as an Imperial Airways pilot to promote the excellence of their aero engines. In it Minchin claimed that he had flown over 100,000 miles on Napier engines. Certainly this may have been possible, because many of the civil aircraft that Minchin flew were powered by the Napier Lion engine. This was a mere six months before Minchin and Barnard's epic proving flight with the new Bristol Jupiter engine.

Throughout the whole of this period I have never had a forced landing from engine failure, or experienced any engine trouble whatever. It is my opinion that the Napier is unquestionably the best aero engine of today. During the whole of my flying experience of thirteen years I have never before experienced such consistent reliability.

No doubt he was adequately rewarded for this tribute.

On 12 October Minchin piloted Sir Samuel[51] and Lady Hoare and Sir Sefton Brancker to and from the Brussels International Air Congress,

AIR MINISTRY,
GWYDYR HOUSE,
WHITEHALL, S.W.1.

14th October, 1925

Dear Col. Minchin

    I did not have an opportunity on our arrival at Croydon on Monday of thanking you for the admirable journey we made from Brussels.

    I was extremely anxious to get back to London as early as possible so it was most fortunate that were no longer delayed by the fog.

    The journey was most confortable in every way and considering how bad the visibility was in some places it seemed to me that we did it in remarkably good time.

Yours truly

Samuel Hoare

Lieut.Col.Minchin,C.B.E.,D.S.O.,
   C/o Imperial Airways Ltd.,
     Croydon Aerodrome,
      CROYDON.

---

[51] Sir Samuel Hoare, later Lord Templewood, was Secretary of State for Air, with a seat in the Cabinet.

flying a DH34. Minchin received a short letter from Sir Samuel Hoare, thanking him 'for the admirable journey we made from Brussels.... The journey was most comfortable in every way and considering how bad the visibility was in some places it seemed to me that we did it in remarkably good time.'

In September Harry went onto half pay with the Royal Navy and took up residence at Annagh. He invited his brother Jack and sister Vi to join him there for Christmas. He wrote later:

I cannot attempt to describe the exquisite pleasure it was to me to see us three together again in the old home after all these years and vicissitudes; 12 years anyhow. Alas, as it happened, it was for the last time. Jack's leave expired on Monday morning in London and we left Annagh in my car on Sunday to catch the Cork Mail at Ballybrophy. As luck would have it, we missed the connection and I had to rush him all the way to Kingstown Pier by 8pm, never having been to Dublin before by road and leaving Ballybrophy at 5pm in the dark. We did it, and I remember my last sight of old Jack, us two standing in the saloon of the SS Munster having a whiskey and soda each as the clock struck eight and I had to go ashore. He was very distrait and it comes to me now: did he get a presentiment that this was our last Goodbye?

98

Chapter Fifteen

The Bloodhound Tests

Late in December 1925 *The Aeroplane* announced that the Bristol Bloodhound (G-EBGG), fitted with the 'highly secret' 450hp Jupiter VI radial air-cooled engine designed by Roy Fedden of the Bristol Aeroplane Company, was coming to Croydon. It would be flown thrice daily between Croydon and Bristol by Lt Col Minchin and Mr FL Barnard, working in relays, in an extended test of its reliability when in regular air service. On 1 May *The Aeroplane* carried a full report on the extended trial, which lasted from 4 January until 8 March and covered 25,074 miles (equivalent to a flight round the world) in 225 hours 25 minutes. The engine was officially sealed in 31 places so that no replacements or adjustments could be made, apart from the routine changing of plugs. Two newspapers reported that 'the engine was running so well at the completion of the tests that the pilot, Colonel Minchin, expressed keen

Minchin and Franklyn Barnard

The Cairo flight 30 June 1926

disappointment at its discontinuance.' In January Sir Sefton Brancker joined Minchin for one leg of the flight.

Just two days after the completion of the Bloodhound tests, Minchin was reported[52] as setting a new record[53] of 86 minutes for the Croydon–Paris trip in the three-engined Handley Page Hampstead W9a (G-EBLE) *City of New York*. And on 8 April he added the Handley Page W10 to his commercial licence.

The Aeroplane of 9 June reported that Minchin had the previous week flown the Bloodhound 400 miles as far as Dijon in very poor weather and, with adverse reports for southern France and Italy, had returned to Croydon to await improved conditions. On 30 June he was off again in the Bloodhound, this time with Freddy Mayer, an engineer from Bristols, in an attempt to fly from Croydon to Cairo in two days. This proved to be the best-recorded of all Minchin's exploits in the air, because Mayer supplied *Flight* magazine in July with a blow-by-blow

---

[52] *British Civil Aircraft 1919-1972* vol 2 by AJ Jackson (Putnam 1973).

[53] It would be almost two years before Arthur Wilcockson on 17 February 1928 reduced the Croydon – Paris record to 80 minutes, piloting the W9a Hampstead G-EBLE (the same machine that Minchin would crash at Westerham on June 1927 while attempting the same record. See page 120).

account of their journey. Leaving Croydon at 0400hrs on the Friday, they reached the aerodrome at Dijon by 0800hrs to find that the wagon with 50 gallon drums of petrol and oil was waiting, but with no means of getting the fuel into the petrol tanks which were on the top wing of the aircraft. Slowly, aided by the petrol company agent, and using cans and funnels, it proved possible to get about 100 gallons into the tanks. They had telephoned the customs agent at Dijon, some five miles away, and he undertook to set out for the aerodrome at once. It was more than an hour and a half before he appeared, riding a bicycle, a cripple who had lost a leg in the war. The shade temperature had already reached 26ºC and they took off without further delay. Climbing to some 12,000 feet to begin their passage of the Alps, they soon met with violent storms and severe bumps. Having both had very little sleep the previous night, both men began to feel the effects. As Mayer recalled:

> As we were approaching this gap [between the mountains] our machine went into a left-hand diving turn . . . The manœuvre surprised me considerably as we were turning off our compass course for . . . no reason. As the engine had not been throttled back during this manœuvre, I rapidly concluded that Col. Minchin was suffering from my own complaint and had fallen asleep. I gave him a push in the back with my foot (Col. Minchin afterwards described it as a kick) to remind him that we were still making for Cairo. Like the good pilot that he is, Col. Minchin first studied the compass, and then turning to me, with his invariable smile, inquired how long we had been off course and immediately set off again in the proper direction.

Emerging onto the hills of northern Italy, they sighted the sea at Genoa and at about two o'clock landed at Pisa where the commandant of the Italian Air Force unit and the Shell representative were awaiting them. The aircraft was fuelled while the two travellers were taken by car to Pisa for a wash, lunch and a half-hour tour of the town which of course included the famous leaning tower. By 1600hrs they were on their way towards Brindisi.

Four hours and 400 miles later they were within sight of the airship sheds at Brindisi, where they found few facilities, no telephone and no assistance. The petrol was there but they had to wait the arrival of the representative of the petrol company who was still in Brindisi ten miles away. As Mayer wrote: 'As a matter of fact Brindisi aerodrome is today practically unused and no one was quite able to understand why we had been instructed by the Italian government that we must land there. As a result there are very few conveniences of any kind.' They soon found that the only food available was a boiled egg each, and some bread and wine. This was in fact the intended supper of the *Maresciallo*, the station warrant officer, who had done his best to help them. Both Minchin and Mayer were desperately tired and when eventually Minchin was able to relax on the officer's bed, he found the room occupied by a swarm of mosquitoes. Rest was interrupted at 0200hrs by the arrival of a *Regia Marina* officer who had been sent to organize the refuelling of the Bloodhound. This was eventually completed under the illumination provided by the headlights of two cars. Customs were satisfied, and by 0515hrs they were at last airborne over the Adriatic and heading for Corfu and Athens. Mayer reported:

> ...this part of our journey was an exceedingly pleasant one. The engine purred along with an unvarying beat and miles of sea were eaten up beneath us, while the island and coastal scenery was in many ways exceedingly fine. On approaching Athens, however, the air bumps were extremely severe. We were bumped and shaken to such a degree that we were mighty glad to feel our wheels touch the aerodrome.

This was at 0900hrs. The Greek officials had everything ready for them: fuel and food and a place where 'Col. Minchin was able to snatch half an hour's rest.'

Leaving Athens two hours later, Mayer noted that 'the monumental ruins of the classic city presented from the air a most impressive spectacle.' Passing over the island of Crete at 1300hrs, he noted:

> Over the sea a slight breeze spread and there was no horizon. During the four hours crossing the Mediterranean not a single boat was seen ... About this part of the trip there was something eerie. One could feel the air flying past and the whistle of the wind as it passed our wires, but minute after minute sped on apparently getting no further on through the volume of haze which was spread out in front and which in its turn merged into the troubled sea.

At Sollum

It was with relief that they sighted the sandy coast of Africa but it was not easy to locate their position. Turning to the west, they sighted a military camp with an aerodrome and, flying low, they spotted an Italian flag. So they turned sharply about and followed an easterly route along the coast until they reached Sollum, still Italian territory. A mile further on was a pile of cans marked Shell. They landed, taxied up to the cans and Mayer went off to find assistance, for there was no ladder, no funnels and no visible help. Soon an Egyptian army lieutenant and a group of Arabs came to help and, in tremendous heat, with the metallic parts of the aircraft too hot to touch, the team poured in the petrol. One Arab, as Mayer recalled, appeared with a tray and three cups of coffee which he insisted be drunk. 'Even now I shudder when I think of the flavour of my first Egyptian-made coffee', he wrote.

With the tanks but three quarters full and darkness falling, they took off once more, heading for Cairo. After half an hour and in near total darkness, Minchin decided that they had to land. He found a small landing place that was marked on their maps and made an excellent landing onto soft sand, striking the tail skid on a partially submerged water pipe. They were met by a British officer, Captain Hillier, and some Egyptian officials who made them welcome and supplied food and accommodation. In the morning, after a welcome night's rest, ropes were

At Mersa Matruh

found and a large party of wildly-excited Arabs proceeded to haul the Bloodhound out of the soft sand onto and along an elevated roadway. Mayer selected a couple of Arabs to turn the airscrew and showed them how to do it. Immediately a swarm of enthusiastic Arabs decided to help and it needed the intervention of Captain Hillier to still the chaos and allow the Jupiter to be started.

Once airborne, they headed for Cairo and, 50½ hours after taking off from Croydon, landed at the RAF aerodrome at Heliopolis. As Mayer wrote: 'the delays at Brindisi and Sollum robbed us of the record that we had set our hearts on making.' After a wash, some food and a cup of tea, Mayer changed the plugs and a mere two hours after landing they decided to begin the return trip. Reaching Mersah Matruh against a head wind, they landed and spent a good night in the Government Rest House, well-protected with mosquito nets. Before dawn they were off again, flying the 150 miles to Sollum against a head wind in two hours. Here the help was better organized than before and the tanks were filled while they had a meal of bread and cheese and coffee. Taking off again they headed for Crete and Athens, Minchin electing to follow the coastal route rather than fly over the Cretan mountains. This added two hours to this leg of the journey which in consequence took 5½ hours in all.

At Athens

Nearing Tatoi aerodrome at Athens at a height of about 2000 feet, 'we found a very fine specimen of eagle close to us.' They had been warned of the danger posed by these birds which had lately caused a Greek aircraft to crash, killing the pilot.

Mayer continued the story:

> It was Saturday afternoon when we landed at Athens and we found the whole of the staff had left for the day. Fortunately the Shell company's representative was there and a few men were available to help us. While the petrol was being put into our machine we were taken to have some food, for which by this time we were more than ready. After a considerable time food arrived, consisting of two small cutlets and some potatoes. . .hungry as we were, we were quite unable to disengage any of the meaty portion from the bone. Another source of supply, however, came to light, namely some cold meat. Colonel Minchin, fearing a repetition of the first course, declined a portion with courtly politeness but I decided at any rate to give the course a trial. While I started on our next journey with a certain amount of content, Colonel Minchin left Athens just about as empty as he entered.

Shell claim the credit

The marketing men at Shell lost no time in claiming credit for Minchin and Meyer's exploit in flying to Cairo and back with this August 18th 1926 advertisement in *The Aeroplane* magazine, although Bristols and the two protagonists received a share of the credit.

They took off and had to climb hard to get over the mountains which rose just north of the aerodrome. They met another large eagle, which caused Mayer to grasp the Very pistol and hold it in readiness.

Their passage over Greece, Albania and Corfu was made difficult by bad storms and bumps. 'The machine was buffeted this way and that and up and down till I positively began to feel nervous.' After crossing the Adriatic they landed at Brindisi, where they found that one tyre had burst and the tail skid was broken. They were greeted by their old friend the *Maresciallo*, who had donned his best uniform in their honour and by 1500hrs on the Monday repairs were complete. But departure had now to wait the arrival of an officer of the Italian Air Service, which meant another night in Brindisi. Explaining that they wished to leave at 0400hrs the following morning, they were assured that the officer would be present before that time. Needless to say, he was not, and it was after 0615hrs before he arrived and they were able to depart.

At Pisa the weather reports delivered the firm message 'flying impossible'. So another night was spent at Pisa and in the morning, despite continuing unfavourable weather reports, Minchin took off, flying across the Gulf of Genoa and Savona to Albenga. So bad was the weather, with thunder, lightning and violent rain, that they returned to Pisa. Here they enjoyed a visit to the Dornier works and inspected the Savoia-Marchetti S55 flying boat in which the Marchese de Pinedo was to attempt a round-the-world flight. The following day they lunched with the Marchese at his villa. One more day was spent waiting for the bad weather to abate. They took off on the following day and travelled due west, passing over Menton, Monaco, Nice, Cannes and Toulon to Marseilles, where they landed. The only food available consisted of five sardines and some bread and coffee which they shared. Moving on again, they flew along the valleys of the Durance and the Rhône, still experiencing bumpy weather and strong head winds which reduced their ground speed to about 50mph. They landed at Dijon and there they stayed the night. Leaving Dijon at six on Saturday morning, they landed at Paris and thence to Croydon, where they landed about noon. In all they had covered 5405 miles in 56¾ hours flying time, an overall average of 95mph.

Hearing that there was to be an aero race at Hendon that same afternoon, they wasted no time in flying there where the Bloodhound, still piloted by Minchin, took part in the race.

Mayer wrote his own postscript to the arduous trip that they had undertaken together:

> *I should not like to close this report without paying a tribute to the piloting of Colonel Minchin. He had a very strenuous test of endurance and pilotage throughout the whole trip, and his airmanship on all occasions proved sound and correct . . . hours at the joystick, flying over such difficult country and over wide stretches of sea must be considered a very fine effort indeed for any air pilot.*

Chapter Sixteen

The Loewenstein Episode

Alfred Loewenstein

Alfred Loewenstein was a Belgian financier and businessman whose fortune, back in the 1920s, was estimated at £100 million. Rumour had it that he was one of the world's ten richest men. From his base at Biarritz he controlled a vast financial network. A man of seemingly inexhaustible energy, at Biarritz he ruled over a private court of some 200 people, all committed to the furtherance of his plans and visions. However there were those who doubted his substance, even his probity. As a captain in the Belgian army during the war, spent as a quartermaster, he emerged, it was said, richer than he began. Appointed Commander of the Bath (CB) by the British government, it was rumoured that this might have been by purchase (the Honours system was in disrepute in the early 1920s). By the summer of 1928 he was engaged in a feud with the Dreyfus brothers, in particular Dr Henri Dreyfus, founders of British Celanese. There was speculation about a £200,000 jewel robbery from his villa at Biarritz and it was said that he was being blackmailed. Still more alarming were rumours that he was in league with Arnold Rothstein, an American mobster and gangland leader, who was known to have fixed the 1918 World Series and to have his finger in Wall Street swindles and political fixes. It was also said that Rothstein and Loewenstein created the modern international drug trade.

None of this was common knowledge when Loewenstein, in furtherance of his hectic lifestyle, negotiated with Imperial Airways the hire of several aircraft and the men to pilot them. Harry wrote 'this man used aeroplanes as you or I would use taxicabs, and he decided to have his own aeroplanes where others would have a motor car or two. Jack was taken on as chief pilot and technical air expert. His pay was enormous and all expenses paid. He flew his millionaire all over Europe – Biarritz, Athens, Monte Carlo, Madrid etc, etc, and enjoyed it hugely.' History is less than clear as to precisely who worked for him and when. It seemed to have begun in the second half of 1926. McIntosh wrote of being one of four pilots seconded to him and of Loewenstein as being 'invariably courteous and reasonable in what he demanded of his pilots. He was a tall, well-built man of about fifty and a most accomplished sportsman.' Gordon Olley also wrote of being appointed Director of Aviation by Loewenstein, of there being eight aircraft in the fleet, and of flying around Europe for him. This included visits to his vast estate at Thorpe Satchville near Melton Mowbray, where he kept a fine stud of horses and had built his own private aerodrome at nearby Croxton. *The Aeroplane* magazine was more explicit when on 1 September 1926 it reported that Messrs Minchin, McIntosh and Olley[54] had been to Biarritz with a W8b and a Vulcan, hired by Loewenstein 'to fly to such places as Berne, Brussels and Barcelona at a hire rate of 6d [2½p] per mile for each seat whether occupied or not.' By the beginning of November McIntosh and Olley must have dropped out because the magazine reported facetiously that the 'Loewenstein Navy', with Lieut Colonel Minchin as Commodore

---

[54] McIntosh and Olley were both less than honest in their memoirs, for neither mentioned the role of the other, nor those of Minchin and Hamilton in the Loewenstein fleet, although McIntosh admits that he was one of a team of four pilots.

Prince Charles D'Orléans
Duc de Nemours

and Mr Leslie Hamilton[55] as First Mate, had arrived in England the week before to make their winter headquarters at Melton Mowbray. On 10 November 1926 *The Aeroplane* reported that the 'Loewenstein Navy' had acquired two more Fokkers, one a triple Lynx and a CV (a two-seater fighter) with a French Jupiter engine which Hamilton would bring to Croydon during the week. Then again on 24 November it stated that Lt Col Minchin (now promoted to 'Admiral' by the journal) flew the owner to Brussels and back in the Fokker FVIIa. According to brother Harry, it was at this time that Minchin met and became good friends with Prince Charles d'Orléans and it was he, Harry insists, who presented his brother with a two-seater open-top Rolls-Royce.

---

[55] Hamilton flew a Vickers Viking IV amphibian (G-EBED), with which he had operated a winter sports passenger service between Croydon, St Moritz and Nice in 1926, and brought this with him to Biarritz. The Viking had been purchased by the Princess Loewenstein-Wertheim and was used by her as a personal aerial taxi.

In December 1926, according to Harry, Minchin 'had hopes of getting over to America to try to fly the Atlantic against two American machines which were also trying to do it. I was naturally tremendously thrilled, but could get no more news out of him, as he was not a very good correspondent.' The challenge of an east-west Atlantic crossing was clearly in his mind, stimulated by the Raymond Orteig prize of $25,000 for the first non-stop flight in either direction between France and the United States. The year 1926 had seen three Atlantic attempts. Leaving Spain on 22 January 1926 Major Franco had successfully crossed the South Atlantic by stages to Argentina in his Dornier Wal flying-boat. On 22 September a trimotor Sikorsky S35, piloted by French fighter ace René Fonck, had crashed and caught fire on take-off at New York, bound for Paris. Then on 17 October 1926 a Brazilian, de Barros, and his crew set out from Genoa in a Savoia-Marchetti S55 to follow the South Atlantic crossing. They eventually arrived on 28 April 1927!

By January of 1927 Minchin was back on routine cross-Channel work and on 13 January he added the Handley Page Hampstead W9a to his commercial licence. By July 1928 Loewenstein had abandoned his hired fleet in favour of a three-engined Fokker FVIIa (G-EBYI) which he had bought from KLM. The aircraft was kept at Croydon and maintained by George Young, the KLM ground engineer. Imperial still supplied the pilot, Donald Drew, and the flight engineer, Bob Little.

On 4 July 1928 Loewenstein arrived at Croydon with his staff of personal secretary, valet and two female stenographers. At the airport and bound for Brussels, Loewenstein was in amiable mood, quizzing Little about the weather and remarking that he planned to be back in England in a week or so. Just after 1800hrs Drew took off and set course before handing the controls over to Little. Loewenstein and his secretary, Arthur Hodgson, sat in front with the two secretaries, Eileen Clarke and Paula Bidalon, behind in rear facing seats. Before they were half way across the Channel, Loewenstein was seen to have removed his jacket, collar and tie. He then placed a marker in the book that he was reading and made his way to the toilet compartment.

Ten minutes passed and Hodgson conferred with Baxter, the valet, who knocked on the toilet door. Hodgson then forced open the toilet door, only to find it empty. The only passenger door, adjacent to the toilet, was ajar. Drew, the pilot, alerted by Hodgson, checked that Loewenstein was

112

Hodgson, Loewenstein and Drew

indeed no longer on board and then circled to explore the area of sea into which his passenger might have fallen. When this proved fruitless, he set the aircraft down on the sandy beach at St Pol, near Dunkirk. This proved to be in a restricted military zone and they were quickly met by a detachment from nearby Fort Mardyk. Drew and Little were free to fly the aircraft to nearby St Inglevert airfield while the rest of the party was taken to Calais. Despite the likelihood of a death by accident or worse, the French authorities were little concerned. The incident had occurred beyond French territorial waters and was of no concern of theirs.

The press found the disaster of immense interest and wild speculation was rife. Loewenstein's wife, Madeleine, travelled from their home at Brussels and visited the aircraft at St Inglevert. She instructed pilot Drew that the Fokker was to be sold without delay and he flew it back to Croydon on 5 July, the day after the accident. There, however, it was impounded pending an Air Ministry investigation while the Fokker company conducted its own investigation, declaring that in flight the door would have needed two persons to force it open. On 9 July Drew and Little were called to attend the official enquiry at Brussels, where they asserted that in an in-flight experiment the door had opened easily. The magistrate concluded that an accident had led to Loewenstein's death and criticized the French failure to mount an investigation. In England the Air Ministry's Inspector of Accidents, a Major JPC Cooper, conducted in-flight tests on the door and, in essence, stated that it could not have been opened by one man alone.

On 19 July, a French trawler found Loewenstein's badly decomposed body, subsequently identified by his watch-strap and denture, dressed in underpants, shoes and socks, in the sea near Cap Griz Nez. An autopsy found that he had sustained a massive stomach wound and that many bones had been broken by the fall from 4000 feet. His body was laid to rest at a cemetery outside Evere, near Brussels, in an unmarked black marble grave. In his 1987 book *The Man who Fell from the Sky*, author William Norris, after exhaustive inquiry, decided that murder had been perpetrated by certain of Loewenstein's staff and pilot Drew, who was having an affair with Loewenstein's wife Madeleine, and that she was behind it. The case was never pursued by the British, French or Belgian police.

Arnold Rothstein, alleged confederate of Loewenstein, was shot dead in a New York Times Square hotel in November 1928. Fred Baxter, the valet, who was on the aircraft, committed suicide in Paris in 1932.

Chapter Seventeen

Transatlantic Mania

Given the prevailing furore regarding transatlantic flight, there can be little doubt that Minchin's ambitions in this direction would have been stimulated by the extravagant enthusiasm which surrounded this endeavour. This was indeed the time when a form of transatlantic mania invaded the aviation world, and even men of normally sound and mature judgement were carried along on this wave of euphoria. Minchin would have been well aware of the knighthoods bestowed on Alcock and Brown in 1919. The conquest of the Atlantic was a heaven-sent opportunity to restore his ailing fortunes.

Apart from the very obvious dangers inherent in the east to west crossing with its fogs and adverse prevailing winds, the still primitive navigational aids, and the need to recruit a capable co-pilot, there remained the most difficult of all, the problem of finding a sponsor who would provide the £4000 to £5000 needed.

Nevertheless the year 1927 saw twenty-two transatlantic attempts, thirteen flying from west to east and six from east to west across the North Atlantic plus three from east to west across the South Atlantic. Only four North Atlantic flights, all west to east, were successful, plus three across the South Atlantic, although two of these were flown in stages. None succeeded in the east to west crossing. Seventeen lives were lost in the year of these endeavours.

On 13 February the Marchese de Pinedo, whose acquaintance Minchin had made during his stop at Pisa en route to Egypt, was the first away in the Savoia-Marchetti S.55 flying boat *Santa Maria*. This leisurely flight wandered down the east side of Africa, across the South Atlantic and north to the Roosevelt Dam, Arizona. There a replacement *Santa Maria* had to be sent from Italy to allow the crew to return to Rome on 16 June, having covered more than 30,000 miles.

Still in February, a Uruguayan, one Larre-Borges, flew from Pisa with his crew in a Dornier Wal, planning to reach Pernambuco in Brazil. After hair-raising adventures following the loss of their aircraft off the shores of North Africa, they were grateful to retire to Italy.

On 16 April Commander Richard E Byrd, later better known for Polar exploration, with a crew of three in a Fokker VII trimotor, crashed on take-off from Roosevelt Field, New York, damaging the aircraft and seriously injuring the chief pilot, Floyd Bennett. On 20 April 1927 CG Grey, the ascerbic editor of *The Aeroplane*, under the heading 'The Atlantic Blues', was caustically critical of these ventures, writing:

> We still have people who are proposing to fly from New York to Paris, and Paris to New York for the Orteig Prize. Why anyone living in dry USA wants to fly to wet Europe and get all mixed up with the Eighteenth Amendment and the Carte des Vins, or alternatively to fly from wet Europe to dry USA and ruin their teeth with iced water and their constitutions with what every self-respecting businessman conceals in a special drawer in his roll-top desk, passes all comprehension. The risk of falling into the intervening strip of water which is salt and undrinkable by both wets and drys does not seem to affect the issue. And in spite of the Sikorsky tragedy of last year we have several individuals preparing to repeat the performance.
>
> After all, the Atlantic has been flown several times now, and nearly everyone is confident that it can be done again . . . and what good is it going to do anyway? All these attempts do is to draw a lot of publicity to individuals long before they are anything like ready to start, and when they crash . . . the public is led to believe that aviation is merely a stunt.

Notwithstanding these strictures (which in any case they will not have seen), on 26 April Lt Cdr Noel Davis and Lt Stanton Wooster in a Keystone Pathfinder crashed soon after take-off from Langley Field, Virginia, and both were killed, just a week before their planned flight to Paris.

On 8 May 1927 French war ace Lt Charles Nungesser[56], with navigator François Coli, set off from Paris for New York in the Pierre Levasseur PL-8 biplane *L'Oiseau Blanc*. Neither they nor their aircraft were ever seen again[57].

---

[56] Nungesser was the French number three ace from the Great War with 45 victories.

[57] A memorial to their memory can be found on the cliffs above the Normandy resort of Etretat. The undercarriage (which they dropped after take-off) is in the Musée de l'Air in Paris.

At 0742hrs on 20 May 1927 Charles Lindbergh, age 25, an unknown airmail and barnstorming pilot, left Roosevelt Field, Long Island, in the *Spirit of St Louis*, a converted Ryan monoplane, to fly the Atlantic. He landed at Le Bourget, Paris, at 22.24hrs the next day, having achieved the first solo west to east crossing of the Atlantic in 33½ hours and incidentally winning the $25,000 Orteig prize. As he taxied in, the darkness became alive; a vast crowd raced towards the aircraft like an advancing tide, shouting 'Lindbergh! Lindbergh!' He was carried from the aircraft on the shoulders of the French crowd. The next day, after spending the night at the American Embassy, he found a huge crowd out front, congratulatory cables and telegrams from all over the world and hundreds of reporters and photographers. For the next few days he was cheered, fêted and lionised.

Some days later, on Sunday 29 May, he took off for Croydon, flying via Brussels. McIntosh, flying a DH50 commissioned by *The Daily Sketch* and accompanied by a photographer, flew with him from Brussels. As he later recalled in his memoirs:

> *Over Dartford a veritable circus of machines joined us and it was quite a mix-up. . . I closed right in on Lindbergh and stuck to him like a leach. There was now Jimmie Youell in the cavalcade, flying a W8b full of sightseers and photographers. Over the Crystal Palace Minchin with the HP Hampstead joined us . . . Over Croydon I could see a mass of cars and a multitude of people pressed up against the hastily erected fencing. Already the field was restricted for landing, but after one exploratory pass we came in together in formation over Plough Lane . . . and landed in the direction of the ADC hangars. Immediately there was a roar as the fences went down and the excited crowd swarmed onto the aerodrome from all directions. Several came within an inch of decapitation by our still revolving propellers . . . The aerodrome could not be cleared by the small squad of police and about thirty aircraft were left circling Croydon, each pilot with an anxious eye on his petrol gauge . . . the Hampstead landed in a recreation field in South Croydon out of petrol and the rest all landed in nearby aerodromes.*

In fact Minchin landed in a cabbage field near Selsdon Road, Sanderstead. George Duff, who worked for Air France at Croydon, recalled the day of

The Handley Page W9a *City of New York*

the landing[58]. George and his friends had been asked to help the police by holding a rope to keep the crowd back. As Lindbergh taxied in, the crowd surged forward and George found himself holding a short piece of rope neatly cut at each end. 'Excited people spread like an ink stain on green blotting paper. A hare broke cover and chaos was complete.' Meanwhile, George recalled, circling overhead in a three-engined Handley Page W9a (G EBLE *City of New York*) was one Colonel Minchin. Short of petrol, he was forced down in a field just south of Sanderstead church. That night George with the local 'bobby' sat on the undercarriage, keeping guard. 'It had seemed to be a straightforward recovery job but when the Colonel arrived the next day he ordered all furnishings and trappings to be removed, lit a cigarette, watched the smoke curl, and said 'I will take her off.' The field was bumpy and uncultivated; trees grew around its sloping edges. 'When I signal, then chocks away', he said. Much easier said than done. The pressure of the machine at full throttle pushed the chocks into the soft ground. At last they gave and away she went, brushing the trees on the far side.' George had shut his eyes.

Minchin had now seen at first hand the hysteria with which the young Lindbergh had been greeted at Croydon. Surely here at last was a way to redeem his fortunes.

---

[58] George Duff's reminiscences were originally recorded by his daughter for *The Old Lady*, the house journal of the Bank of England and in 2001 reprinted in the Journal of the Croydon Airport Society.

Chapter Eighteen

Still It Goes On

Leaving New York on 4 June 1927 in a Wright-Bellanca WB-2 *Miss Columbia*, Clarence Chamberlin and owner Charles Levine, a millionaire scrap dealer, succeeded in crossing the Atlantic. They left from Roosevelt Field, New York, and landed at Mansfeldt, a suburb of Eisleben, 110 miles south west of Berlin, having covered 3911 miles. Had it not been for some last minute contractual issues concerning Levine, which delayed the take-off by some days, the *Miss Columbia* might well have won the Orteig prize.

By the time of Lindbergh's epic flight Minchin was already deeply involved with McIntosh, his colleague from Imperial, in a scheme to purchase a new Fokker for £3000. McIntosh in his memoirs says: 'I made up my mind to have a go if I possibly could. The early weeks and months went by in a turmoil of worry and frustration. But by the Spring things were far enough advanced to seek an aircraft and co-pilot.' Their intention was to fly in August from London Northolt to New York and, after an eight hour break, to fly back again. There is on record a telegram of 10 June to Minchin from Fokexport which said: 'If definite decision

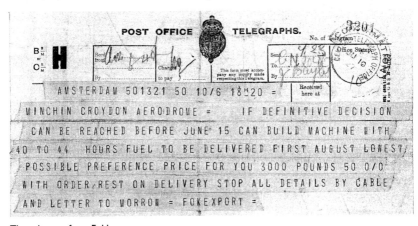

The telegram from Fokker

can be reached before June 15 can build machine with 40 to 44 hours fuel to be delivered first August. Lowest possible preference price for you 3000 pounds 50% with order rest on delivery. Stop. All details by cable and letter tomorrow.' On 20 June their proposed partnership was reported by the London *Evening News* which waxed eloquent about their experience as flyers and quoted McIntosh as saying:

> We do not think there is anything in the project beyond a question of airplane reliability. We shall take turns as pilots, and will try to beat the long distance record on the return journey from New York. . . A thing we flying fellows would like to get out of the ordinary man's head is the idea that we are heroes. A London bus driver gets more thrills trying to carry, say, as many passengers through the streets of London as I have carried across the Channel.

The *Daily Express* on 21 June took up the tale, suggesting that the flight would begin from RAF Cranwell where the runway had been specially lengthened. The two men succeeded in raising £2000 (Lord Inchcape's daughter, the Hon Elsie MacKay, and an American, William B Leeds, were among their backers) but then abandoned the project through an inability to raise the remaining £2000 needed to complete the purchase and cover other costs. Strangely, McIntosh makes no mention of this venture in his memoirs, written some thirty-six years later[59].

Possibly it was Minchin's next adventure which brought the partnership to an end. On 27 June 1927, piloting the W9a Hampstead on a routine flight from Paris to Croydon, he ran out of fuel and had to land the aircraft in a field at Cudham, near Westerham. The large aircraft narrowly missed a house and struck some trees, damaging the starboard wings and undercarriage. Neither the crew of two nor any of the nine passengers was injured. This was Minchin's second accident in the Hampstead in a month but this time it was treated with some gravity. The Air Ministry Accident Investigations Branch reported on 17 August. They found that:

> The pilot was very experienced, having served with distinction in the Royal Air Force during the War and flown as a Civil pilot in the service of Imperial Airways for over three years . . . his flying

---

[59] Given also McIntosh's penchant for recalling slightly malicious anecdotes about Minchin, it could be wondered whether he nurtured some lingering recollection of a far-distant dispute.

The crash at Westerham

*time on the Air Routes amounted to about 1600 hours. He flew the
aeroplane in question between London and Paris on five occasions
during the ten days preceding the accident.* It went on: *weather
conditions on the day were fair, with visibility not less than five
miles. The pilot started on the flight at 1200hrs, 25 minutes after
another aeroplane had left Le Bourget for Croydon. The aeroplane,
an Argosy, did not reach Croydon until 1413hrs and was therefore
overtaken by the Hampstead. The Channel was crossed at a height
of about 1200 feet and the aircraft continued on its course at about
this altitude, with each engine running satisfactorily, until it was
over hilly country north of Sevenoaks. The starboard engine then
abruptly ceased to fire and the next moment the other engines
failed in a similar manner. The pilot then headed the aircraft
towards the only field which offered any prospect of a successful
landing, but at the last moment, finding that he had insufficient
height to clear some trees, he was obliged to turn to the right and
alight in a small field. The pilot succeeded in landing the aircraft,
but after it had run for about 40 yards on the ground the starboard
planes came into collision with some trees . . . the pilot failed to
make use of the Fuel Economiser and throughout the flight this
control lever was in the position for maximum Rich Mixture .
. . the accident was due to errors of judgement, amounting to
carelessness, on the part of the pilot, in that he (1) flew the aircraft
at a speed considerably above the normal cruising speed, (2) failed
to make use of the fuel economiser, and (3) failed to keep watch on
the amount of fuel in the tanks.*

The minutes of the Imperial Airways Board meeting of 19 July 1927
recorded Minchin's dismissal, with the rider that his reinstatement
would be considered after his forthcoming transatlantic flight. This
flight was not the proposed partnership with McIntosh but an entirely
fresh venture with a new team and sponsor.

We have already referred to the friendly rivalry that existed between
Minchin and Raymond Hinchliffe (see page 91). This was probably at
the root of the Hampstead crash[60]. Hinchliffe's log reveals that he was

---

[60] The Hampstead was repaired at Croydon using HP Hyderabad parts and by October was back
in service.

The Vickers Viking amphibian, the Princess in the foreground, Hamilton in the rear cockpit

the pilot of the Argosy that Minchin overtook, notwithstanding that he had taken off in Paris some 25 minutes before Minchin and actually landed at Croydon some 13 minutes after the crash. His log reports succinctly: 'Two engines gave trouble. Minchin crashed in G-EBLE with 9 passengers and was dismissed.'

Still the quest to cross the Atlantic went on. On 29 June Commander Richard Byrd with a crew of three (two pilots and a radio operator) repeated his attempt to fly in the Fokker VIIA/3m *America* from Roosevelt Field, New York, to Paris. Twice they passed over Paris in dense fog, and finally on 1 July turned back to ditch 300 yards offshore at Ver-sur-Mer, just east of Arromanches on the Normandy coast. The crew got ashore using a rubber life raft and the aircraft was later salvaged and returned to the USA.

Meanwhile Minchin, out of a job, had linked up again with Leslie Hamilton, his colleague from the 'Loewenstein Navy'. Irishman James

Fitzmaurice[61], in his unpublished personal diary, records that:

Whilst in London, I met my old friends Minchin[62], Leslie Hamilton and Frank Courtney. They were busily engaged organizing an attempt on the east-west crossing and I invited them to use Ireland as their take-off base . . . I invited Minchin and Hamilton to come over to Ireland and inspect Baldonnel aerodrome as a possible take-off ground. Leslie owned a Vickers Viking amphibian[63] and they promised to fly over to Dublin. I duly received a telegram informing me they were leaving London and would arrive in a few hours. They actually arrived a week later.

It appears that after taking off from Croydon they suddenly remembered something that was engaging their attention in Dover, so they altered course for the Channel and the White Cliffs. There they ran out of money and gave joy rides at 10/- [50p] a time to raise the finances to pay their hotel bills and secure supplies of petrol and oil. They had worked their way in this fashion round the south coast of England and up into Welsh Wales. This had been the cause of the delay. They landed on Baldonnel on 26 July in the amphibian Viking with the retractable undercarriage down. Upon taxying up the tarmac I noticed the three seats were occupied by Minchin, Hamilton and a very dear old RAF friend of mine, 'Cod' Foster, who was home on leave from Mesopotamia. They all wore Jack Tar type sailor hats one buys at Woolworths for kids' parties, and very large horn-rimmed toy sun glasses. As they shut off the engine Hamilton, who was in the pilot's cockpit, shouted, 'Let go the anchor.' Minchin, who occupied the front seat out in the nose of the machine heaved the sea anchor out on to the tarmac shouting 'Aye, Aye, Sir.' Such was the carefree manner[64] in which they were entering their hazardous undertaking. It was the real spirit of the old RFC: eat, drink and be merry for tomorrow you

---

[61] Fitzmaurice was Commandant (Major), second in command of the Irish Air Corps and had served with the 17th Lancers, the West Surrey Regiment, the King's Liverpool, the RFC and the RAF. He later partnered McIntosh in his failed Atlantic attempt in September 1927 and still later, in April 1928, achieved the first successful east-west crossing (see pages 150-151).

[62] 'Fitz' wrote later in the diary: 'Lieut Colonel Freddie Minchin had served as my Wing Commander during the war.' This would have been 6 Wing during September-November 1919. (See page 61)

[63] Hamilton had brought this aircraft with him when he joined Loewenstein's fleet.

[64] McIntosh had it that they would then ask, in an American accent, 'Say, youse guys, is this England?'

*die. They spent a few rollicking days with us in Dublin and started
back to London. They assured me they were satisfied with Baldonnel
and would use it for their take-off.* (They actually flew on to inspect
the beaches at Clifden in County Galway, the most westerly spot in
the British Isles.)

By 5 August, the press had got onto the venture and several newspapers
published identical accounts:

*Mr Leslie Hamilton and Lieut Colonel F.F.Minchin, the Imperial
Airways pilot, who are attempting a non-stop flight from Ireland
to Ottawa in a Fokker-Jupiter monoplane, will fly to Amsterdam
tomorrow to take delivery of their Atlantic machine, and they hope
to start on their Atlantic flight on August 15th. They have now
decided to begin their flight from Baldonnel Aerodrome, near Dublin,
owing to the lack of facilities at Clifden in the west of Ireland, where
they originally intended starting. Lieut Colonel Minchin will fly
the machine from Amsterdam to Bristol via London on Saturday
(6 August) and, after the Bristol engine has received its final tuning,
they will fly to Baldonnel. Their intention is to fly to Ottawa and then,
refuelling, start back immediately to Europe, making for Vienna in
an attempt to break the world's non-stop long distance flight record of
3905 miles set up by Chamberlin and Levine.*

Meanwhile the Atlantic quest went on. Germans Baron von Hünefeld,
of North German Lloyd, Capt Hermann Köhl of Luft Hansa and Junkers
test pilot Fritz Loose, a Czech, in a modified all-metal Junkers W33
named *Bremen*, together with an identical aircraft called *Europa*, manned
by Cornelius Edzard and Johan Risticz with Hearst reporter Hubert R
Knickerbocker, set out on 14 August from Dessau. The *Bremen* was soon
forced to return to Bremen and was badly damaged. The *Europa* did
much better but also was obliged to return, landing at Dessau after 23
hours in the air.

On 17 August Edward Schlee and William Brock left Harbour Grace,
Newfoundland, in a Stinson Detroiter *Pride of Detroit*, on a planned
round the world flight. They reached Croydon 23 hours and 2358 miles
later and continued to Tokyo where they were arrested as spies and their
aircraft seized. They abandoned the flight.

Chapter Nineteen

The Transatlantic Flight: Preparations

The Princess

Meanwhile Minchin and Hamilton had found a backer, and it may be that this helped to precipitate Minchin's withdrawal from the partnership with McIntosh. Leslie Hamilton had for some time acted as aerial chauffeur to the Princess Ludwig zu Loewenstein-Wertheim-Freudenberg, more commonly known as the Princess Loewenstein-Wertheim. Born Lady Anne Savile in 1865, she was the daughter of the fourth Earl of Mexborough and had married Prince Ludwig zu Loewenstein-Wertheim-Freudenberg in 1897. The Prince lost his life in the Philippine War of Independence in 1899, since when the Princess had pursued an independent life[65]; an athlete and a feminist, even an inventor, she had flown in the face of her family's opposition to her escapades. Beginning in 1912, she took flying lessons at the Beatty-Wright school at Hendon and became the first woman to fly across the Channel, albeit as a passenger, and later took part in pioneer long distance flights. Although she had undergone tuition, there is no record of

---

[65] The *New York Times* stated in 1913 that she was 'a frequent visitor to New York and a familiar figure in certain circles of New York society.'

The Princess with Leslie Hamilton

her gaining a pilot's licence and as early as 1914 she was employing an aerial chauffeur, one Roland Ding. She had a tendency to dress flamboyantly and consequently was something of a figure of fun in aviation circles. The Princess lived at Ditton Lodge[66], Thames Ditton, and worshipped at St Raphael's in Kingston-upon-Thames, a beautiful Italianate Roman Catholic church built in 1848 by her great uncle, Alexander Raphael, sometime Sheriff of London. St Raphael happened also to be the patron saint of aviators.

Leslie Hamilton, born in London on 26 October 1898, had been commissioned into the Royal Engineers in 1916 and transferred to the Royal Flying Corps early in 1917. He learned to fly in Egypt and on 30 March 1918 joined 17 Squadron in Macedonia[67], moving to the new 150 Squadron on its formation on 1 April 1918. The citation to his DFC, gazetted on 8 February 1919, spoke of his gallantry and skill and said that he had brought down, or helped to bring down, six enemy machines. After the war ended, he was retained by the RAF as a flying instructor[68] and in September 1922 piloted a DH9c (G-EBAX) with the Princess as passenger in the King's Cup[69] Air Race, finishing sixth. He was awarded the MBE in June 1923 and resigned his commission in September 1925. *The Aeroplane* in March 1925 reported that he might be joining Imperial.

---

[66] Ditton Lodge is now a fashionable hotel.

[67] This was a week or two after Minchin relinquished command of 47 Squadron in Macedonia.

[68] He was reputed to have taught Jim Mollison to fly.

[69] For the 1923 King's Cup the Princess hired C D Barnard to pilot her DH9C (G-EBDD).

COLONEL F. F. MINCHIN.   PRINCESS LOWENSTEIN-WERTHEIM.   CAPTAIN L. HAMILTON.

Minchin, Princess Loewenstein-Wertheim-Freudenberg and Leslie Hamilton

Then in January 1926 he appears to have acquired a Vickers Vulcan Type 61 which was by May lost at sea off Italy. In July 1926 the magazine reported that he would be piloting a Martinsyde F6 biplane (G-EBDK) at the Lympne Air Meeting on 1–3 August. Since then he had gained a reputation as 'the aerial gypsy', chauffeuring the Princess in her Vickers Viking amphibian, running a winter sports passenger service between Croydon, St Moritz and Nice and, by September, working for Alfred Loewenstein, and then generally 'odd-jobbing' around Europe using the Viking amphibian. Not content with this, beginning on August Bank Holiday 1927, he had begun using the Viking to deliver the *Daily Mail* each morning from Southampton to Jersey.

Freddie West, VC, whom we shall meet later, knew him well and recalled that:

> *He was handsome, dark and debonair . . . bubbling over with vivacity, always gay, and on top of that he had this dare-devil flying reputation – enough to make any girl swoon. He played the piano beautifully – mostly jazz in those days, but he could play anything... He was a man with no conceit in his make-up.*

That Hamilton was the Princess's protégé as well as preferred pilot seems clear. Hamilton and Minchin had worked together, almost certainly for the first time, while with Loewenstein. So, given both the Princess and Minchin's expressed desire to fly the Atlantic, it is not surprising that

The St Raphael leaving Holland

the three came together as an aspirant Atlantic team. Indeed it has been suggested[70] that the venture had been agreed at a dinner party at the Savoy hosted by the Princess and attended by the two pilots.

With the Princess's financial backing, the purchase of a new Fokker FVIIa monoplane from Holland was negotiated by Minchin. This would be fitted with a single 450hp Jupiter VI air-cooled engine designed by Roy Fedden, chief engineer of Bristols – similar to the one that Minchin had tested so exhaustively back in 1926. Most of the ten-seat passenger space would be filled with eight cylindrical petrol tanks holding nearly 800 gallons which would give a flying time of about 42 hours and a range of up to 4000 miles. The fuel would need to be hand-pumped into the main wing tanks. The distance by great circle route to Ottawa, their intended destination, was quoted as 3600 miles. Clearly there would not be a great margin of safety. The aircraft was to be painted blue with the wings yellow and a small inflatable boat (but no radio) would be carried.

On 15 August Minchin and Hamilton flew to Amsterdam in the Vickers amphibian to collect the new Fokker which would be registered G-EBTQ. They flew back to Croydon, landing briefly at Ostend due to low cloud

---

[70] *Great Mysteries of the Air* by Ralph Barker (Chatto and Windus 1966).

The St Raphael at Croydon

and mist. At Croydon they were given a black kitten for luck by Imperial typists, after which they flew on to Filton for final checks and tuning by the Bristol Company. This included the replacement of the original aluminium propeller with one made from ash and the installation of navigational instrumentation. These included a Vickers-Reid control indicator which was designed to keep the aircraft on a set bearing, any deviation causing red or green warning lights to flash. This instrument was in use on all Imperial Airways machines. A novel feature was the installation of three magnetic compasses in an equilateral pattern. Until this moment the newspapers were reporting that their intention was still to fly from Baldonnel, near Dublin. However by 24 August it became clear that they had decided on using the RAF aerodrome at Upavon in Wiltshire as their departure point. Hamilton was quoted as saying that 'it was most probable that they would start across the Atlantic tomorrow morning [25 August].'

But on 25 August the two pilots were greeted with the news that the Air Ministry had refused to grant an airworthiness certificate owing to faulty construction of the rudder and tailplane which were similar to those of a Fokker which had crashed recently[71]. Bracing wires were fitted

---

[71] A similar KLM Fokker FVIIa had crashed near Sevenoaks on 22 August when the fin and a part of the rudder fell from the aircraft. The pilot was injured and a mechanic killed.

The St Raphael leaving Filton

Above and left, Minchin and Hamilton

by the mechanics at Bristol and this delayed their departure from Filton until the following day.

Shortly before take-off from Filton on 26 August, Hamilton gave the *Bristol Times and Mirror* representative a message addressed to the citizens of Bristol:

> *On leaving Bristol, I desire to express my thanks for the interest that has been taken here in the venture in which Lieut Colonel Minchin and myself are embarking. We have every confidence that the Bristol-built Jupiter engine with which our monoplane is equipped will carry us over the Atlantic and back again.*

Taking off from Filton at 1615hrs, they wore lounge suits and trilby hats and were accompanied by Bristol engineer Freddy Mayer, who had flown to Egypt and back with Minchin in July 1926, and an American newspaper journalist. The aircraft had been named the *St Raphael*, the patron saint of aviators and, perhaps more significantly, the Princess's mother's maiden name and that of her church at Kingston-upon-Thames. The aircraft made a circuit of the aerodrome at Filton, came back over the hangars and, flying just above the roofs, dipped in salute to the cheering crowds there. The flight to Upavon took just 30 minutes. A reporter from *The Bristol Times and Mirror* described the event:

> *The pilots made a wide sweep over the country in their flight and while over Bristol they came down to an altitude of seven or eight hundred feet, and thousands of people ran into the street or their gardens to watch the big blue monoplane passing over the city.*
> *The plane was flying no higher than 500 feet over Yate, Chipping Sodbury and Hawkesbury-Upton, and charabancs were stopping on the road in order that passengers might witness the passage of a machine that promises to make history in crossing the Atlantic non-stop for the first time in a westerly direction.*

Chapter Twenty

Upavon

We are indebted to PR Reid, the biographer of Freddie West, VC CBE MC, who had won the Victoria Cross in the late war, for an eye witness account[72] of the preparations for the take-off of the *St Raphael*. West had lost a leg in the war but remained in the RAF and was now adjutant at the Upavon station, which was commanded by Wing Commander Vernon Brown[73], Minchin's former schoolfellow. West was deputed to look after the two guests and their aircraft.

Meeting Hamilton in the mess, he asked him,

What chance do you think you have got?

Hamilton replied:

Not more than fifty per cent. Keep this to yourself, but honestly, I think we shan't make it.

Why are you doing it then?

Because it's worth it even if we fail. We've been teamed up together for three months . . . If one of us cracks, the show is off and I couldn't stand the comeback . . . It's all in very good hands and they're not mine. Minchin is the brains behind it all and he's dead keen. I'm only present to take over when he gets tired and I can do that in my sleep . . . don't tell anyone else what I've told you. With Minchin I'm always as keen as mustard. He doesn't know how I feel at all. So keep this to yourself.

What about the Princess – Princess Lowenstein?

I don't believe for a moment she intends to come with us. She's in it for the publicity – the notoriety it gives her.

---

[72] *Winged Diplomat* by PR Reid (Chatto 1962).

[73] Later Air Commodore Sir Vernon Brown, CB, OBE, Chief Inspector of Accidents 1937–52.

West went on:

> *Minchin spent his time putting the finishing touches to his*
> *preparations. His tall, gaunt frame could be seen around the hangar*
> *at all hours. He dressed as if he was going to his office in London. He*
> *was an awfully nice fellow, quiet and unassuming, speaking with*
> *a gentle voice. His eyes were deep brown and his hair black and he*
> *wore a heavy black moustache. He must have been well in his forties.*
> [He was actually 37]. *I have hardly met a more earnest individual*
> *in my life. He was completely dedicated to the venture. He was a*
> *good engineer beside being a good pilot, and he knew what he was*
> *up against . . . Minchin had courage. He told me 'I'm just a cog in*
> *the wheel of England's progress through time. The job's got to be*
> *done by someone and it happens to have come into my hands. I can*
> *only do my best. If Providence is with us, we'll get over; if the wind's*
> *against us – well, someone else will try and win. I only hope it's an*
> *Englishman and not that b . . . Levine.'*

On August 30, Winston Churchill, Secretary of State for Air, during an official visit to witness army manoevres on Salisbury Plain, called to inspect the *St Raphael*.

Later Hamilton reported that the Princess had been on the phone. It was to say that Levine, the American millionaire, was nearly ready to leave in *Miss Columbia* and there was no time to be lost. This was a piece of imaginative, even spurious, information designed to encourage Minchin to fly sooner, rather than later. Levine's Fokker had been impounded and placed under guard in Paris by the authorities after a dispute with M. Drouhin, his pilot. Levine, who was not a pilot, had hoodwinked the Paris authorities and, on 29 August, had taken off alone and flown the aircraft to Croydon where, after four abortive attempts, he managed to make a clumsy landing. So Levine, with Ray Hinchliffe, was now at Croydon with the Fokker which the next day they flew on to Cranwell for remedial work and further tests. They were by no means ready to fly the Atlantic. In fact they never did and it was not until 23 September that they set off eastwards, eventually reaching Rome.

The Princess also claimed that the weather reports were favourable and that she wanted to leave the next day, 31 August. Hamilton was despondent. 'It's a confounded nuisance the Princess looks like coming along . . . She's worth fourteen gallons of petrol, nearly an extra hour in the air . . . I'm afraid it's goodbye to all this, goodbye to my family. Goodbye to old England, and the RAF boys.' The Princess's motivation is worthy of note: she desperately wanted to be the first woman to fly the Atlantic. Levine at that time was planning to fly with a wealthy young American, Mabel Boll, nicknamed the 'Diamond Queen'. She also intended to be the first woman to fly from Europe to New York and had offered $25,000 to anyone who would take her.

It might be wondered why Minchin and Hamilton both accepted the Princess's dubious information without question.

Then another piece of news reached Upavon. McIntosh had found a backer and a co-pilot, Minchin and Hamilton's friend, James Fitzmaurice. They had acquired an aircraft and were flying from Rotterdam to Lympne en route for Ireland.

In fact McIntosh had found a philanthropic American, William Leeds, to finance the venture. He had purchased a one year old Fokker F.VIIa from KLM for 39,921 Dutch guilders, which he named *Princess Xenia* after his sponsor's wife. The airline had made the necessary modifications and fitted long range fuel tanks in place of passenger accommodation. He was already at Filton with the *Princess Xenia* where a Jupiter engine and navigational instrumentation were being fitted prior to departure for Baldonnel.

There was a send-off party in the mess that evening, wives as well as officers crowding into the ante-room. Hamilton was at the piano. He played a favourite, a hit from a current West End show[74], whose cast he had entertained at his London flat. He played it wistfully, several times. The song was called 'My Heart Stood Still':

> *I took one look at you,*
> *That's all I meant to do,*
> *And then my heart stood still . . .*

Minchin went to bed at midnight, but not before writing a poignant last note to his brother Harry:

---

[74] *A Connecticut Yankee* (Rogers and Hart).

Dear old Henry,

Just a line to tell you we are off to fly the Atlantic tomorrow, at least we are going to try, so in case something happens you are my best friend in the world, everything I have is yours, no sob stuff but the best of luck to you, you have always been the best of brothers to me.

I think we have every chance of success or I should not be such a B.F. as to start, anyway if I do you can take it from me I won't do so badly out of it and I may make some money.

All the best old Boy. I will wire you when I get there.

Yours ever, Jack.

I think we have every chance of
success or I shouldn't be such a
B.F. as to start, any way if I do
you can take it from me I
won't do so badly out of it
& I may make some money.
All the best old Boy I will
write you when I get there

Yours ever.

Jack.

Harry wrote later that his brother was 'worn and haggard from overwork and sleepless nights.' Meanwhile, in the nearly empty mess, Hamilton remained at the piano, a glass in his hand and a cigarette between his lips. He was urged to get some rest. 'There'll be plenty of time to sleep when we get there', he said, 'and a permanent rest if we don't.'

At 0400hrs on Wednesday 31 August 1927 the two men met in the Mess ante-room, sipping coffee, surrounded by a group of pilots. It was a beautiful dawn, with clear skies and a ground mist. The two airmen checked out the take-off run by car, at its maximum 1300 yards, and then used the mess telephone to say goodbye to their families. The *St Raphael*

Goodbye

was wheeled out of its hangar and set facing west, while wooden supports were placed under each wing to support the enormous weight of fuel. Engineers from Bristols tested the aircraft's engine. A strong east wind had sprung up and, while this might help with petrol consumption, it was not ideal for a heavily-laden take-off.

A smart Rolls-Royce drove up to the mess entrance. It was the Princess, dressed in mauve-coloured riding breeches, a leather jacket of the same colour, high-heeled riding boots with fur edging and a black straw hat with a brim that covered her ears. She was quite heavily made up. Her luggage consisted of two attaché cases, a small wicker food basket and two hat boxes. There was also a wicker armchair, her seat in the aircraft. Escorted to the mess by West, she asked for a cup of strong coffee, whispering 'I would love some brandy in it.' 'Do you really mean to go with them?' asked West. 'Well, I'm dressed for it', she replied.

Soon a second car drew up at the mess and out stepped a Bishop, the Roman Catholic Archbishop Mostyn of Cardiff, dressed in his vestments, no doubt summoned by the Princess. With him came two

St Raphael ready for take-off

priests, Fathers O'Reilly and Vallnet, from the parishes of Tidworth and Devizes. The party set off for the hangar.

The aircraft was now out of the hangar and all the station staff had gathered to watch the take-off. The Bishop prayed and blessed the aircraft and sprinkled holy water on it. He took each man by the shoulders and wished him good luck and God-speed. The Princess knelt to receive the Bishop's blessing. 'God bless you all', he said. 'May you have a safe journey. We will not forget to pray for you.'

The reporter from the *Bristol Evening News* later wrote:

> *Colonel Minchin was cool and collected. He smiled goodbye to his friends and got into the St Raphael with as much concern as if he was entering a motor car for a joy-ride.*

The man from the *Daily Express* added:

> *Colonel Minchin wore a well-cut lounge suit, white collar, dark tie and soft brown hat, which he laid carefully aside to be worn on landing. His moustache was as well groomed as on any ordinary day, and his whole manner spoke of calm and a keen desire to go on with the job. Asked what he thought of his chances of success, he paused for fully a minute before replying: 'Do you think I would go if I did not think I was certain of arriving there? Everything is in our favour. The wind is right, the weather is splendid, and our monoplane is in perfect trim. I cannot prophesy any time for my journey. It may only last twenty hours, but it may last for forty. We are prepared for all eventualities.'*

Asked for a last message to the women of England, the Princess said,

A Solemn moment

The blessing

The final take-off

'Tell them I am proud of the honour, and I pray that it will be an Englishwoman who will be first to cross the Atlantic from this side. I am confident and I am unafraid. I have confidence in the pilot and in the machine.'

Hamilton had been violently sick behind the hangars and, according to West, was deathly pale, his eyes ringed and bloodshot. 'This is a grim ordeal', he kept saying, 'This is a grim ordeal.' Bidding West good-bye, he added, 'here's £25, all my spare cash. Will you give it to the mechanics who've been working on the *St Raphael* with my thanks and best wishes? It's better they have it than the fishes. Goodbye, old man, and thanks for all you've done for us.'

The three flyers climbed into the aircraft and Minchin ran up the engine. Many spectators feared that the heavily laden Fokker would never get airborne but would crash, a fiery inferno, somewhere down the runway.

West escorted the fire engine and ambulance to the far south-eastern end of the aerodrome at a spot known as Jenner's Firs and stopped on a narrow chalk road some two feet below the level of the plain. A low barbed-wire fence marked the boundary of the aerodrome. He watched the take-off with binoculars and saw the *St Raphael* trundle slowly across the field and almost imperceptibly gather speed. As the aircraft neared the edge of the airfield, it was still glued to the ground. West shouted

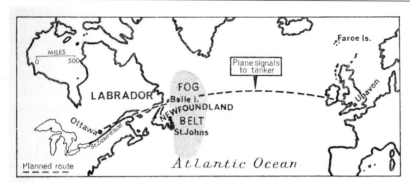

Minchin's planned route

to his men: 'Stand by! It looks like trouble.' He and his party threw themselves flat on the ground while the *St Raphael* passed overhead four feet above the road, missing the barbed-wire fence by inches. 'My God, Minchin', he shouted in relief. 'Well done, Minchin! You certainly knew how to cut things fine.' He now appreciated why Minchin would sit for hours at a desk in his office, poring over his calculations – worrying things like a terrier.

The time was 0730hrs. The aircraft rose slowly and disappeared westwards at about 300 feet. Twenty-five minutes later it flew low over Filton, exactly on course.

Chapter Twenty One

The Final Flight

Minchin followed a course which would take him over the South Wales coast. The *St Raphael* was sighted at St Ann's Head, Pembrokeshire at 0920hrs. Captain Harvey of Bargy Castle, Co. Wexford, reported seeing it at 10.15 travelling northwest by west at about 500ft; later it was reported at New Ross at 1020hrs and later over Thurles, Tipperary, at about 1040hrs. Schoolgirl Bridie O'Brien was there at Annagh:

> *It was school holidays and my sisters and brother and I were playing outside. At mid-morning a throbbing noise could be heard coming from behind the church tower. Looking over the woods we saw the dark shape of an aeroplane flying low. In 1927 an aeroplane was a rare sight in Coolbawn and it was flying so very low and slowly. As we watched, it turned, and flew back over the lake, over Islandmore and vanished beyond Galway shore. Colonel 'Jack' Minchin was saying 'Hail and Farewell' to Annagh and Murroughboro' before voyaging out into the bleak Atlantic in an attempt, with his two companions, to be the first flyers to cross the great ocean from east to west.*

At Inverin in County Galway the aircraft was seen by Civic Guards at 1210hrs and it was watched by hundreds of farmers and fishermen as it sped out over the Atlantic between Garumna Island and Inis Mór, the most northerly of the Aran Isles.

The next and indeed last authentic sighting came from the *Josiah Macey*, a tanker owned by the Standard Oil Company, in mid-Atlantic, bound for Germany. This was at 2144hrs GMT on Wednesday 31 August, the day of take-off. The position was latitude 53.50, longitude 20.45.5, which indicated that the aircraft had covered nearly 900 miles since leaving the Irish coast at an average speed of 85mph against headwinds. The ship's crew signalled to the *St Raphael* with an Aldis lamp and received in acknowledgement a series of flashes from the aircraft. The tanker's radio operator sent out a message reporting the sighting, which was picked up by a wireless station on the Irish west coast and relayed to the Air Ministry in London. A direct flight to Ottawa was still possible, though Minchin had a contingency plan to land at Harbour Grace in southern Newfoundland, where a line of oak barrels had been saturated with oil so that the airfield could be kept floodlit all night. Another vessel, the Holland-America steamer *Blij Dendijk* en route for

SEEN WHEN HALF
WAY ACROSS

NEWS OF ATLANTIC AIRMEN
RECEIVED

STEAMER'S WIRELESS MESSAGE

MYSTERY OF LIGHT OFF THE
AMERICAN COAST

THREE OTHER FLIGHTS FAIL

The "Irish Independent" is able to announce to-day that the monoplane St. Raphael, in which Col. Minchin and Capt. Hamilton, with the aged Princess Lowenstein-Wertheim as passenger, set out for Canada on Wednesday morning from Upavon, Wiltshire, was seen when half-way across the Atlantic.

A wireless station on the Irish coast has received a message from the master of the Josiah Macy, a steamer owned by the

Rotterdam from Norfolk, Virginia, and some 420 miles east-south-east of New York, sighted a white light, probably belonging to an aircraft, heading eastwards. This was at 0600hrs GMT. This was very unlikely, all but impossible, to have been the *St Raphael.*

At Ottawa great preparations were being made in readiness for the arrival of the three aviators. The Prince of Wales (later King Edward VIII) and his brother Prince George (later the Duke of Kent) were in Ottawa and postponed their departure. Hamilton's former wife, divorced some two years previously, arrived from New York hoping for a reconciliation if the flight was successful. An all-night vigil was kept along the coast, flares were lit and hundreds of cars lined the airfield at Lindbergh Field, near the Ottawa Hunt Club on the Bowesville Road. Powerful floodlights, searchlights and rockets were prepared to guide the flyers. Fog, treacherous, opaque Newfoundland fog, was banking up across the ocean and drifting inshore.

By midday on 1 September the fog had cleared but there was still no sign of the *St Raphael.* Crowds continued to gather, as did photographers and journalists, and the hope was that they might have landed unseen in the fog. Darkness fell, the night wore on and slowly the crowd dispersed. By morning it was clear that there was to be no triumphant arrival. They might have force-landed in the wastes of Labrador; they might have been picked by a ship which carried no radio. Hawker and Grieve had alighted alongside a tiny Danish coaster, the *Mary,* in May 1919 and nothing had been heard of them for six to seven days. The best that could be hoped for was that they had made a forced landing somewhere short of Ottawa, possibly at Harbour Grace, Newfoundland, where crowds had assembled and a row of oil-saturated barrels had been installed so that the airfield could be illuminated..

So what may have happened? The Fokker was a well-tried machine; the tail unit had been specially strengthened under Air Ministry guidance. The Jupiter engine was well reputed, tuned to concert pitch, and had run sweetly for at least 14 hours. The hand pumping of the fuel tanks was a potential source of problems[75]. In any case their fuel would have been exhausted soon after midnight on 2 September. So if

---

[75] McIntosh wrote later of 'the [fuel] valves [of the Fokker] not working very well' and of the difficulty of working out a foolproof scheme for management of the fuel and a simple sequence of adjustments.

the winds had been as adverse as was believed, they could never have made Ottawa but might just have reached Newfoundland. Could the south-westerly wind have blown them off course so that landfall was made further north somewhere in Labrador, one of the most remote, most sterile and inhospitable voids in the world? If so, even the most intensive search might not find them.

It could be suspected that they may have perished by fire. Both men, according to many photographs, were inveterate smokers. The cabin would have been full of petrol fumes. One carelessly struck match would have turned the *St Raphael* into a firebomb.

Back at Croydon, anxious crowds had started to gather and journalists were busy. An Imperial Airways official was reported as stating that: 'Minchin is one of the finest civil pilots the world has ever seen. He would never lose his head in any circumstances; in a difficult situation Minchin is the man. Minchin is one of the most popular pilots at Croydon and a charming man in every way. Everybody here has the greatest faith in his skill as an airman.' Levine, Minchin's rival, interviewed by the *Daily Telegraph* late on 31 August said: 'I admire Minchin and Hamilton very much for starting their flight in the face of unfavourable weather conditions. But if anything terrible should happen to them I should hate to think that I might have been the cause of their hastened departure. Good luck to them – they are both jolly good fellows.'

At Coolbawn in Tipperary, a telegram for Harry Minchin arrived from nearby Nenagh. It said: 'Delighted to hear Master Jack safe. Nora.' Delivered to 'the Commander', as Harry was known, at Annagh Lodge, it was a sad piece of misinformation from the unidentified Nora.

In Ottawa, JA Wilson, Canadian Director of Civil Aviation, decided against instituting a full-scale search; the Newfoundland Government soon followed suit and decided not to search for the *St Raphael* and its occupants. Informed opinion in Canada and Newfoundland gave their chances of survival or rescue in the frozen wastes as being virtually zero, even should they have succeeded in crossing the coast.

The world's press waxed eloquent about the fate of the *St Raphael* and its occupants. Speculation was rife. The aircraft might have come down in the ocean or it might have landed in a deserted spot in Newfoundland, Labrador or Canada:

*Few people have any idea of the terrible country they would meet in
Newfoundland. A third of it consists of lakes. They might have passed
over the coast, which would almost certainly be wrapped in fog but
inland there are peat bogs for miles, and no-one lives there from
March to November except a few very hardy trappers. Detours around
lakes would take whole days. For food there are plenty of fish, if they
could catch them, and caribou if they had a rifle. They might be in the
country for a week and . . .never be heard of again. Labrador is even
worse and more sparsely populated.*

Within a few days the world had accepted that Minchin and his two
colleagues had been lost, almost certainly at sea.

On 6 September Air Vice Marshal Sir Sefton Brancker, a good friend
of Minchin's, was quoted in the *Irish Times* as saying:

*We cannot stop people from attempting to fly the Atlantic, and we
do not want to stop them. All our great achievements have involved
danger and death in the early stages. Let these pioneers go on.*

And the following day in the *Daily Mirror*:

*The flight from east to west has to be done, and it is idle to talk
of prohibiting the attempt. You can no more prevent a man from
attempting to fly the Atlantic than you can prevent him from
attacking Mount Everest. I could have put money on Minchin
getting across safely.*

On 9 September Sir Sefton Brancker wrote to Harry Minchin:

*I have been hoping against hope that we might have heard
something about your brother before this. I am going abroad
tomorrow, I feel I must write to you before I leave.*

*I knew your brother well, both in and out of the service – and have
frequently flown with him. He is one of our most dashing and gallant
pilots and if indeed he has not been saved, his death will be a serious
loss to British aviation. It was typical of him to push off as quickly as
he did – he was determined not to let Levine get away in front of him
– and we shall at least have the consolation that he died in a fine effort
to maintain the magnificent reputation of British aviation.*

In addition I have lost a friend who cannot easily be replaced.

On 14 September CG Grey penned in *The Aeroplane* what was in effect an obituary tribute:

> *Everybody liked Sq.Ldr.Minchin, he had much personal charm and a kindly nature. He was admired for his skill and courage as a pilot. And during the war 1914–18 he proved himself to be a very good commanding officer. But, somehow, in civil life, he seemed to fail to find a job worthy of his war record or of his social position.*
>
> *Personally he struck one as a man possessed by some constant sadness, so perhaps his end has been welcomed by him. At any rate he died in the course of a great adventure, in which – as those who knew him will agree – neither vanity nor the desire for gain had any part.*

The idea that Minchin might have welcomed death, and have taken two companions with him, seems little more than journalistic hyperbole. But Grey was notorious for that sort of writing.

Apparently undeterred by the fate of Minchin and by a severely cautionary message from Sir Sefton Brancker, Robert McIntosh and James Fitzmaurice took off from Baldonnel aerodrome at 1330hrs on 16 September, bound for America. All went well until at about 1830hrs weather conditions deteriorated so much that the two pilots decided to turn and race for home. They landed on the beach at Ballybunnion and the following day flew the aircraft back to Baldonnel. This spelled the end of McIntosh's Atlantic ambitions, though Fitzmaurice, as we shall see, went on the following year to make the attempt again.

There were six more attempts before the year ended[76]. All were unsuccessful and more lives were lost. Charles Levine, with Ray Hinchliffe, eventually took off from Cranwell on 23 September, but in an easterly direction bound for Karachi. After several vicissitudes, their endeavour came to an end at Rome airport when the engine failed.

Then on 29 September a slip of paper bearing the message:

> S.O.S. We are in waste near Newfoundland
> St Raphael – *Colonel Minchin*

was found in a small bottle on the coast among seaweed in the Gulf of Morbihan, Southern Brittany. The French Direction de l'Aeronautique dismissed it as a hoax as the current would have taken several months to drive the bottle to the French coast.

---

[76] Gunston et al list as many as twelve.

A similar find took place on the shore at Rhode Island, USA, on 8 May 1928 when a fisherman found a whisky bottle containing a pencil-written note which said:

> Captains Hamilton and Minchen [sic] had a quarrel over course. Struck water and sinking fast. Can see light in distance, think off Block Island. Everything out of order now. Ship good for a few seconds yet –Princess Löwenstein.

This also was dismissed as a hoax.

On 13 March the following year, 1928, Minchin's former friend and colleague at Croydon, one-eyed Ray Hinchliffe, partnered by the Inchcape heiress the Hon. Elsie MacKay, took off from RAF Cranwell bound for America in the Stinson Detroiter *Endeavour*. After a sighting off the Irish coast, they were never seen again.

It was not until April 1928 that an aeroplane succeeded in crossing the Atlantic from east to west, when Minchin's friend, Irishman James Fitzmaurice, flew with two Germans, Baron von Hünefeld, and Hermann Köhl, in the Junkers W33 *Bremen* from Baldonnel in Ireland to force-land on Greenly Island off Labrador[77].

On 7 May 1928 the *Portsmouth* [Ohio] *Daily Times* reported that diamonds and other jewels worth approximately $200,000, the property of Princess Lowenstein-Wertheim, were lost on her ill-fated transatlantic flight. Friends of the late Princess said that they consisted of many family heirlooms which she treasured dearly. Therefore she decided to take them with her. In aviation circles, the story is that the jewels were taken with hopes of selling a few of them in the United States in the event that the adventurers needed cash. This is denied, but Prince Charles Philippe, duc de Nemours, who knew all of the late fliers, told the Associated Press correspondent that Captain Hamilton told him of a scheme to make money on the other side. The proposition, as Hamilton outlined it to the Duke, was this: Before starting Hamilton

---

[77] Fitz and his two German colleagues were given a tremendous reception in New York, reputedly by more than two million people, greater even than that accorded Lindbergh. After similar celebrations in Canada, Berlin, London, and finally in Dublin by an enormous crowd of well-wishers, Fitz was promoted Colonel by the Irish government but was hurt by this faint praise. A business venture was destroyed by the Wall Street Crash, he was divorced by his wife and his life entered a slow downward spiral. During World War Two he ran a servicemen's club in London and in 1965 he died, alone and in ill health, in a small bed-sitter in Richmond, Surrey.

bought 600 one-pound notes. His idea was that as the Saint Raphael landed in America all the notes would be autographed by the Princess, Colonel Minchin and himself and sold for $25 to $30 each or for whatever price they might bring in the souvenir hunters' market.

A year after the *St Raphael* was lost, on 3 September 1928, the Icelandic newspaper *Morgunbladid* reported that an aeroplane wheel had been found on the south coast of Iceland bearing the inscription Palladium Cord Aero Standard 1100-220, Nr.106009 and 7.27. A French factory which produced aero wheels confirmed that the wheel was from the British Fokker FVIIa G-EBTQ named *St Raphael*. Other reports have referred to a wicker chair being found on the shore but this has not been confirmed.

There exists an undated (c.1928-30) and unreferenced newspaper cutting in the Minchin album which says: 'The body of an unknown airman was washed ashore yesterday in a cove on the Port au Prince peninsula, on the west coast of Newfoundland.' Enquiries in Newfoundland have failed to uncover any further information about this finding.

Minchin Lake and Wertheim Lake, near to Thunder Bay in Western Ontario, were, a while after these events, so named by the Canadian authorities.

Some time after the tragedy there was erected in the now disused Kilbarron Church of Ireland church at Coolbawn a commemorative plaque which reads:

Sacred to the Memory of
Frederick F Reilly Minchin
CBE, DSO, MC
who perished in the first attempt ever
from England to America
together with
Capt Leslie Hamilton MC
and Princess Anne
of Loewenstein Wertheim,
daughter of the 4th Earl of Mexborough
2nd September 1927

The plaque was later donated by Mrs Alice Gloster to Nenagh Heritage where it is on display. Despite its several errors of fact, this is a moving tribute to three valiant people who so nearly made aviation history.

For some years the belief persisted in some quarters that the *St Raphael* flight was a foolhardy exploit, even something of a stunt. This view was reinforced in Collinson and McDermott's 1934 book *Through Atlantic Clouds* in which they wrote:

> *In reviewing this flight in the light of after events, one is inclined to the opinion that the venture was undertaken in somewhat a light-hearted manner, and that over-confidence rather outweighed routine methods as regards the ordinary precautions that might possibly have been more fully observed. Some doubt, too, has been expressed as to whether sufficient petrol was carried to ensure a margin of safety in case of adverse winds and possible faults in navigation.*

What a marvellous thing is hindsight!

Norman Macmillan, whom Minchin had met in Calcutta in 1922, recalled in his 1967 book *Wings of Fate* a dream that he had had on the night of Minchin's last flight. He saw an aeroplane in the darkened water, partly submerged. The main plane was level with the surface and the fuselage was partly submerged. Two men were swimming around it, trying to extricate

The Coolbawn plaque

153

someone from the interior. 'They did not succeed.' In the morning he told his wife: 'I'm afraid Minchin has gone … Drowned.'

The 1920s were the era when spiritualism and a belief in the paranormal were at their height. Ray Hinchliffe, according to a widely respected medium, one Eileen Garrett, was apparently sending very specific and believable messages to his widow Emilie. He also spoke of the *St Raphael* party: 'I saw Hamilton. I believe they had a terrible time. Everything was true. They turned back and got as near as in sight of the Irish coast. Hamilton said they never had a hope and they caught fire. I saw them. They had struck very bad weather conditions.' A sceptic might point out that Hinchliffe had lived on for six months after Minchin's death. Later Alfred Loewenstein, Sir Sefton Brancker (who lost his life in the R101 disaster in 1930) and others from the R101's crew all passed messages through the same medium.

Practical people will dismiss these phenomena. They are though a part of the Minchin story.

Chapter 22

Epilogue

Minchin's downward path began when he resigned his RAF commission. In the RFC and the RAF he had found success and respect. But he feared the tedium of peacetime service and, as promotion beckoned, of an increasingly deskbound job. Perhaps he felt that he was intellectually inadequate, even temperamentally unsuited, for the sort of role that would be his in the post war RAF. For his temperament was mercurial, restless, and at times irresponsible. He would have been very aware of this.

Away from the inherent discipline of service life, or at least wartime service life, he was at the mercy of his inner daemons, those impulses which drove him to personal and professional disaster. By July 1927 he was under suspension by Imperial, told that his reinstatement depended on his succeeding in the Atlantic attempt. He had no income and was probably broke and in debt. When a wealthy sponsor came on the scene, he would have felt that he had little alternative but to make the attempt. Photographs confirm that he was desperately tired and under strain. Freddie West had thought that he was 'well in his forties', even though he was only 37.

He swallowed the Princess's exaggerations about Levine apparently without question and disregarded the doubtful weather forecasts. Yet, with his contacts at Croydon and elsewhere, he could, with a telephone call or two, have resolved these issues. But he allowed himself to be bullied into an early take-off – with the tragic consequences that befell not just him but his two companions as well

Apart from the two memorial plaques, there remain two physical mementoes of Jack Minchin. In the RAF Museum at Hendon there is a uniform tunic bearing the label

Hetherington's
MILITARY OUTFITTERS
465 YONGE ST. TORONTO

which bears his Lieutenant Colonel's rank badges, the ribbons of his orders, decorations and medals, PPCLI lapel badges and a 'Canada' shoulder flash. There is evidence that the tunic was originally rank-badged on the sleeve and that this was later skilfully altered to the post 1916 shoulder position. The museum also holds his orders and medals (illustrated). These items are not currently on display. They are our last tangible relics of the man remembered in this book.

Minchin's tunic

Let us close the Minchin story with a naïve but affectionate tribute from a fellow airman which makes very clear the regard in which he was held.

```
                    M I N C H I N .
                    _____


                    By a Brother-Aviator.
_____

                He's an absent minded beggar
                and his weaknesses are great
                        That's MINCHIN.

                But He's tried to fly the 'Lantic
                Wiping something off a slate.
                        That's MINCHIN.

    Poor old Dan.

            Lieutenant-Colonel, C.B.E., D.S.O., M.C. and Bar.

    One of the bravest men who ever lived.
    Cool, calm (absent-minded) always.
    One who wanted to keep our heads high when others seemed to be
    winning; when the initiative in progress seemed to be leaving the
    Old Country.

                        _____

            '   He was arrested, once by the Police, when he had
    been having a "Joy-Party" with some of his old War time pals.

                He was pushing his car down the road,
                A Policeman arrested him --
                "Drunk in charge of a car".

    Dan, typical of his good open self, never flinching from facts,
    answered "Yes, Officer, If you say I'm bottled, I'll agree;
    I am pushing my car because I can't drive it".

                The Magistrates saw his point, they agreed, the Police
    said that, not only had they the greatest admiration for
    Colonel Minchin, but his behaviour throughout had been correctness
    itself and entirely as a gentleman, as he was.
                The pity there are not more.

                        _____

    They went off ------- The "Princess" clinging to her religion
    and banking on it to the last; the boy Hamilton on the verge
    of hysteria "It's a grim business" he kept repeating.

                Dan, calm, cool and collected; like his illustrious
    countrymen, Lord Roberts and Lord Charles Beresford.
                Prepared, knowing the possibilities (which the others
    only guessed at) still calm, collected and unafraid.

                        _____

                Dan has gone, please God he has not, he may yet be
    found.

    If he has gone; no one can imagine more fully than the writer
    the final scenes, with Dan, still calm, collected and unafraid,
    watching the others and knowing the worst.

                We hope he may be found.   Dan cannot be spared.
    So far there are few, if any, to replace him as a type.

            MINCH, OLD BOY, COME AND HAVE A LAGER.
```

157

Bibliography

Books

–, *Burke's History of the Landed Gentry of Ireland*, 1904

Allen, Sir Peter, *The 91 before Lindbergh*, 1984

Andrews, C F, *Vickers Aircraft since 1908*,

Barker, Ralph, *Great Mysteries of the Air*, 1966

Barnes, C H, *Handley Page Aircraft since 1907*, 1976

Beatty, David, *The Water Jump*, 1976

Blake, W T, *Flying round the World*, 1923

Bowyer, Chaz, *RAF Operations 1918-38*, 1988

Cole, Christopher and Cheesman, E F, *The Air Defence of Britain 1914-18*, 1984

Collinson, C and McDermott, F, *Through Atlantic Clouds*, 1934

de Watteville, Col H, *The Waziristan Campaign 1919-20*, 1925

Dickson, Charles C, *Croydon Airport Remembered*, 1985

Dixon, Charles, *The Conquest of the Atlantic by Air*, c.1931

Ellis, Frank, *Canada's Flying Heritage*, 1981

Ellis, Frank and Ellis, Elsie, *Atlantic Air Conquest*, 1963

Falls, C & Becke, A F, *Military Operations in Macedonia, 1914 to1919*,
    in two volumes, 1933

Fennelly, Teddy, *Fitz and the Famous Flight*, 1997

Franks, Norman, *First in Indian Skies*, 1981

Franks, Norman and O'Connor, Mike, *Number One in War and Peace*, 2000

Fuller, John G, *The Airmen who would not Die*, 1979

Gibbs, Sir Gerald, *Survivor's Story*, 1956

Gunston, Bill et al (eds), *Chronicle of Aviation*,1992

Halley, J J, *The Squadrons of the Royal Air Force & Commonwealth 1918–1988*, 1988

Henshaw, Trevor, *The Sky their Battlefield*, 1995

Heydemarck, H, *War Flying in Macedonia*, c.1920

Higham, Dr Robin, *Britain's Imperial Air Routes, 1918–1939*, 1960

Hodder Williams, R, *PPCLI 1914-1919*, 1923

Jackson, A J, *British Civil Aircraft 1919–1972*, 1973

Jackson, Archie, *Old Pilots, Bold Pilots*, 1998

Jefford, C G, *RAF Squadrons*, 2001

Johnston, E A, *Airship Navigator*, 1994

Jones, H A, *Over the Balkans and South Russia 1917–1919*, 1923
Jones H A & Raleigh, Sir W, *The Great War in the Air*, 1928
Joubert de la Ferté, Sir P, *The Fated Sky*, 1952
King, Peter, *Knights of the Air*, 1989
Learmonth R, Nash J & Cluett D, *The First Croydon Airport 1915-28*, 2nd edition 1977
Lewis, Cecil, *Sagittarius Rising*, 1994
MacCarron, Donal, *A View from Above*, 2000
Macmillan, Norman, *Best Flying Stories*, 1941
Macmillan, Norman, *Freelance Pilot*, 1937
Macmillan, Norman, *Wings of Fate*, 1967
McIntosh, R H, *All-Weather Mac*, 1963
Moolman, Valerie, *Women Aloft*, 1981
Nevin, David, *The Pathfinders*, 1985
Norris, Geoffrey, *The Royal Flying Corps: A History*, 1965
Norris, William, *The Man Who Fell from the Sky*, 1987
O'Brien, Bridie, *How We Were*, 1999
Olley, G P, *A Million Miles in the Air*, 1934
Orange, Dr V et al, *Winged Promises*, 1996.
Owen, H Collinson, *Salonica and After*, 1919
Penrose, Harald, *The Adventuring Years 1920-1929*, 1973
Penrose, Harald, *Wings across the World–An Illustrated History of British Airways*, 1980
Reid, P R, *Winged Diplomat*, 1962
Rosenbaum, Robert A, *Aviators*, 1992
Rowe, Percy, *The Great Atlantic Air Race*, 1977
Samson, C R, *Fights and Flights*, 1930
Seligman, B J, *Macedonian Musings*, c.1920
Shaw, M, *No. 1 Squadron*, 1986
Stroud, John, *European Transport Aircraft since 1910*, 1966
Williams, Jeffery, *Princess Patricia's Canadian Light Infantry*, 1972

Journals
Cross and Cockade International Journal
Croydon Airport Society Newsletter
Flight
Saga Magazine
The Aberdeen Press
The Aeroplane
The Bristol Evening News
The Bristol Times and Mirror
The Daily Express
The Daily Mail
The Daily Mirror

The Daily Telegraph
The Eastbournian
The Eastern Press
The Evening Telegram (Newfoundland)
The Guardian (Ireland)
The Irish Independent
The Irish Times
The London Gazette
The Manchester Despatch
The Montreal Daily Star
The Nenagh Guardian
The Northern Whig (Belfast)
The Notts Journal
The Observer
The Offally Chronicle
The Portsmouth [Ohio] *Daily Times*
The South Wales News
The Star
The Sunday Express
The Sunday Graphic
The Sunday Times
The Times
The Western Daily Press
The Western Mail
The Westminster Gazette
The Yorkshire Telegraph

Illustration credits

See page iv

81	Bristol Aero letter	Minchin album
82	Joubert letter	Minchin album
84	W8b Handley Page	AJ Jackson collection
85	Minchin 1924	Minchin album
86	Croydon caricature	Charles C Dickson
88	Minchin in cockpit	Croydon Airport Society (James Jeffs Collection)
93	Crash at Carville	Minchin album
93	Crash at Carville	Croydon Airport Society (James Jeffs Collection)
94	At Croydon 1927	Minchin album & Croydon Airport Society
96	Napier advert	*Aeroplane* magazine
97	Samuel Hoare letter	Minchin album
99	Minchin and Barnard	*Flight* & AJ Jackson Collection, Minchin album
100	Mayer and Minchin	*Flight* & AJ Jackson Collection
103	At Sollum	*Flight* & AJ Jackson Collection
104	At Mersa Matruh	*Flight* & AJ Jackson Collection
105	At Athens	*Flight* & AJ Jackson Collection
106	Shell advert	*Aeroplane* magazine
109	Alfred Loewenstein	*Illustrated London News*
111	Prince Charles D'Orleans	Taponier, Paris
113	Hodgson, Loewenstein & Drew	The Press Association
118	HP W9a Hampstead	*Flight*
119	Telegram	Minchin album
121	Crash at Westerham	AJ Jackson Collection
121	Crash at Westerham	AJ Jackson Collection
123	Viking amphibian	Croydon Airport Society (James Jeffs Collection)
127	Princess	Minchin album
128	Princess with Hamilton	Ralph Barker
129	Minchin, Princess & Hamilton	Minchin album
130	St Raphael leaving Holland	Minchin album
131	St Raphael at Croydon	Minchin album
132	Minchin and Hamilton	Ralph Barker, Minchin album
133	St Raphael leaving Filton	Minchin album
133	Minchin and Hamilton	Ralph Barker
138/9	The last letter	Minchin album
140	Goodbye	Croydon Airport Society
141	St Raphael ready for take-off	AJ Jackson Collection
142	A solemn moment	Newspaper cutting (unknown)
142	The Blessing	Newspaper cutting (unknown)
143	The final take-off	Ralph Barker
144	Map	Ralph Barker
145	Newspaper cutting	Minchin album
146	Newspaper cutting	Minchin album
153	The Coolbawn plaque	The Nenagh Heritage
155	Medals	James Kostuchuk
156	Tunic	James Kostuchuk
157	Tribute	Minchin album

Index

Suffix 'n' denotes a footnote; 'p' an illustration

Charterhouse School 67
Chipping Sodbury 134
Chipstead 165
Chittagong 76, 77
Christ's Hospital 10
Churchill, Winston 136
Clarke, Eileen 112
Clifden 92, 125
Cobham, Alan 95
Coli, François 116
College of Heralds 22
Collier, 2Lt 58
Collinson and McDermott 153
Cologne 2, 89, 91
Colombo 74, 77
Colquhoun, Lt 28
Connaught, Duke of 21
Connaught Rangers 1, **11–16**
Connecticut Yankee, A 137
Cooch Behar, Maharajah of 75
Coolbawn 145, 148, 152, 153p
Cooper, Major JPC 114
Corfu 102, 107
Cottier, Lt ER 48
Courtney, Frank 95, 124
Cranwell 120, 136, 150, 151
Crete 102, 104
Cricklewood 83
Crown Hill, Croydon 87
Croxton 110
Croydon 2, 75, **83–98**, 99, 100, 101, 104, 107,
   111, 112, 113, 117, 118, 120, 122, 123, 124,
   125, 129, 130, 131, 136, 148, 151, 156
Croydon Airport Society 90, 118n
Crystal Palace 117
Cudham, Westerham 120
Cummings 76
Curragh, The **12–13**, 15
Curtiss Company 17n
Curtiss:
   JN-3 44
   NC–4 flying boat 91
   Pusher 1910 type 17, 20

D
d'Orléans, Prince Charles 111, 151
Daily Express 120, 141
Daily Mail 129
Daily Mirror 149
Daily Sketch 117
Daily Telegraph 148

Daimler Airway 83, 84, 89n
Dakka 67
Dartford 117
Daurs 65
Davis, Lt Cdr Noel 116
Dawes, Lt Col GWP 51
de Barros 112
de Lesseps, Ferdinand 37n
de Pinedo, Marchese 107, 115
de Watteville, Col H 68
Delhi 67
Dera Ismael Khan 66, 69
Dessau 125
DH (Airco):
   DH1 44, 46p
   DH2 55, 56
   DH4 83
   DH9 66, 75, 76, 81, 83, 92, 128
   DH10 66, 95
   DH18 84, 89n
DH (De Havilland):
   DH34 84, 85, 86p, 89, 90, 91, 92, 98
   DH50 89, 91, 117
   DH66 Hercules 96
Diamond Queen 137
Dickebusch 26
Dickson, Charles Couper 86p
Dickson, Lt 58
Dijon 100, 101, 107
Ding, Roland 128
Direction de l'Aeronautique 150
Dismore, Freddie 85
Ditton Lodge 128
Dodd, CF Wolley 85, 96
Dojran 51, 53, 56
Dojran Memorial 57n
Don 33
Dornier Wal 112, 116
Dornier works 107
Douai 33
Dover 61, 124
Drew, Donald 112, 113, 114
Dreyfus, Dr Henri 110
Drouhin M. 136
Dublin 4, 73, 98, 124, 125, 131, 151
Duff, George 117–118
Duke of Kent 147
Dum Dum 75
Dunkirk 113
Durance Valley 107
Durham 92

E
Eastbourne 14, 16
Eastbourne Aviation Company 14
Eastbourne College **7–10**, 71, 91
Eastbournian, The 10, 71
Edmonton Pipe Band 22
Edwards, Lt Col Ivo 75, 79
Edzard, Cornelius 125
Egypt 34, **35–50**, 52, 67, 95, 115, 128, 134
El-Arish 38, 43, 44, 45, 47, 48, 50, 92
El-Baiga 46
El-Kharari 44
El Mashalfat 48
Ellis, Frank 17n
Etretat 116n
Euston Station 82
Evening News 120, 141
Everard, Alfred 82
Evere 114

F
Fairey IIIC seaplane 76
Farman:
    F.60 Goliath 89n
    Série 11 Shorthorn 37
Farnborough 34
Farquhar, Lt Col Francis 21, 22p, 28, 30
Farrow, 2Lt WH 56
Fated Sky, The 41n
Fedden, Roy 99, 130
Fenton, 'Bird' 13
Fielden, Major Jack 74
Filton 131, 133, 134, 137, 144
Fitzmaurice, James 124, 137, 150, 151
FK3 52, 53
FK8 52n, 54n
Flanders 26, 35
Flieger Abteilung 300 41, 44
Flight 38, 39, 40, 44, 57, 59, 62, 74, 100, 127, 145
Fokker 33, 34, 50, 111, 112, 113, 116, 119, 123, 125, 130, 131, 136, 137, 143, 147, 151
Fokker:
    CV 111
    E1 *Eindecker* 33
    F.VIIa 111, 112, 123, 130, 131n, 137, 152
    F.VIIa *Princess Xenia* 137
    F.VIIa *St Raphael* 130, 131p, 133p, 134, 135, 136, 139, 141, 143, 144, 145, 146, 147, 148, 150, 152, 153, 154
    F.VIIa/3m *America* 116, 123

Fokker Scourge 34
Fonck, René 112
Fordham, Lt HA 47
Fort Mardyk 113
Foster, 'Cod' 124
Fowler, Frederick Bernard 14
Franco, Major 112
Freelance Pilot 75n
Freeman, Capt RH 50
Freeman, ACM Sir Wilfred 50n
French, Sir John 26
Frezenberg Memorial 21
Frezenberg Ridge 21

G
Galss 47
Galway 92, 125, 145, 146
Gardner, Major GD 59
Garrett, Eileen 154
Garumna Island 146
Gault, Major Hamilton 21, 22p, 23, 30
Gaya 75
Gaza 50
Genoa 101, 107, 112
Georgie, Aunt 29, 31, 72
Gererat 48
Gloster, Mrs Alice 152
Gnome rotary engine 14
Goeben, [SMS] 58, 59
Goodfellow, Capt Alan 53
Gorgop 55
Gosport 37
Gotha 55
Graf Zeppelin 83
Grand Couronné 60
Grandvilliers 89n
Grange Road, Eastbourne 7
Great Mysteries of the Air vii, 130n
Greece 107
Greenly Island 151
Greenwich, RNC 7
Grenfell, Lt EO 32p
Grey, CG 116, 150
Greyhound Hotel, Croydon 89
Grosvenor Gardens, Victoria 82
Guilfoyle, Lt WJY 47
Gulf of Genoa 107
Gulf of Morbihan 150
Gunner 25
Gunner and Gillson 77
Gunston et al 150n

Mikra Bay 52
Miles, William V 17
Mills, Wing Cmmdr RP 68
Minchin, Brian iv
Minchin, Capt Charles 3
Minchin, Caroline Royds Lloyd 'Lena' 6, 16, 25, 72
Minchin, Denis iv
Minchin, Falkiner John 'GP' 4, 7, 43
Minchin, FFR 'Jack', 'Dan' or 'Freddie'
 1 Squadron 31–34; 14 Squadron 35–50; 47 Squadron 51–60; 52 Wing 65–69; 89 Wing 62–63; Bankruptcy 82; Bloodhound tests 99-108; Canada 17–22; CBE 72; Childhood 4–10; Civil Aviation 80–108; Connaught Rangers 11–16; Dismissal 120–122; Divorce 77, 91; DSO 58; Engagement 71; France 26–30, 31–34; Imperial Airways 80, 85–98; India 65–69, 75–77; Learning to fly 14–15; Lindbergh 115–118; Loewenstein 109–114; Maidstone 61–62; Marriage 73; MC 43, 50; PPCLI 21–30; Sandhurst 11–12; Transatlantic flight 127–153; Transatlantic preparations 115–116, 119–125, 127–143; Wing Commander 61–64
Minchin, Gen Frederick Falkiner 4
Minchin, Henry Falkiner 'Harry' 4, 5p, 6, 7, 10, 11, 14, 15, 16, 24, 25, 29, 41, 43, 62, 71, 72, 73, 74, 75, 77, 79, 80, 82, 90, 91, 92, 95, 98, 110, 111, 112, 137, 138, 139, 148, 149
Minchin, Humphrey, 24n
Minchin, Violet Marjorie 'Vi' (Mrs Abbott) 5p, 6, 98
Minchin Lake 152
Minnie, Aunt 25, 29
Miss Columbia 119, 136
Mollison, Jim 128n
Monaco 107
Moneygall 3
Montague, 2Lt PD 57
Montreal 22
Morane Parasol 33
Morgunbladid 152
Mosquito, The 52n
Mostyn, Archbishop 140
Mudros 59
Murraghboro' House 4n, 72, 79, 145
Mursley Grange, Winslow 71, 73
Musée de l'Air, Paris 116n
Mustabig 50

N
Napier 96, 97
Nasrullah 65
National Archives 37, 54, 81
Nenagh 148, 152
Netheravon 32
Neuve Chapelle, Battle of 33
Newfoundland 92, 125, 146, 147, 148, 149, 150, 152
New Ross 145
New York 100, 112, 114, 116, 118, 119, 120, 123, 127n, 137, 147, 151
New York Times 114, 127n
Nice 107, 111n, 129
No 1 General Hospital, Le Havre 27
Norfolk, Virginia 147
Norris, William 114
Norris Mansion hotel, Haymarket 80, 90
North West Frontier 72
Northcliffe, Lord 92
Northolt 119
Norway, Neville Shute 83
Nungesser, Lt Charles 116

O
O'Reilly, Father 141
O'Brien, Bridie 145
O'Malley, Charles 18
Old Carthusian, Handley Page V/1500 66-67, 92
Old Lady, The 118n
Old Pilots, Bold Pilots 90n
Olley, Gordon 85, 89n, 110
Ottawa 21, 22, 26, 125, 130, 146, 147, 148
Over the Balkans and South Russia 54
Owen, H Collinson 59

P
Palestine 39, 95
Palladium Cord Aero Standard 152
Parabellum guns 33
Parachinar 66
Paris 2, 90, 91, 95, 100, 107, 112, 114, 116, 117, 120, 122, 123, 136
Pathans 65
Penrose, Harald 85n
Pernambuco 116
Peshawar 66, 68
Petit Couronné 56
Pfalz EII 41
Philippine War of Independence 127
Pierre Levasseur PL-8, L'Oiseau Blanc 116

[

Albatross

Treecreeper

Gnatcatcher

Lapwing

Shearwater

Night Heron

Swift

Stormpetrel

Thrasher

Typical Owl

Waxwing

Godwit

Sparrow

Longspur

Lark & Thrush

]